The book that you *don't* read
won't help.   JIM ROHN

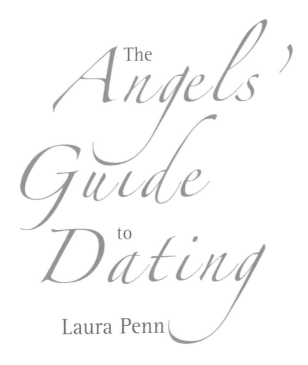

The
Angels'
Guide
to
Dating

Laura Penn

Illustrations by Matthew Usmar Lauder

QUADRILLE

For Margaret and Dickie and their romance.

Contents

Every blade of grass has its *angel* that bends over it and whispers, "*Grow, grow.*"

THE TALMUD

INTRODUCTION

Dating is a bit like hang-gliding: Exciting, great fun, but also very dangerous. It requires a leap of faith into the unknown and there's always the possibility of getting hurt. The difference with dating is that, if at first you don't succeed, you can always try again. If you are a would-be dater you may feel swamped by the deluge of advice coming at you from magazines, chat shows, and so-called "relationship experts," but inevitably this advice is man-made and therefore fallible. Wouldn't it be better to get help direct from heaven?

"The angels can help.
The angels can help."

Say this to yourself like a mantra, because it is true.

The snag is that the angels can only help you to find love if you ask them to. They never interfere, but they can (and do) intervene if you ask. And, let's face it, if you are looking for love you'll probably need all the help you can get, so having an angel in your pocket is a great idea.

Whether you consider yourself to be a loner, a learner, or a loser in love, let the angels guide you through the maze of emotions from the thrill of the first date to the heartache of being dumped. The angels can help you enjoy each and every moment of dating ... even the bad ones.

People often ask how they can contact their angels. Is there a celestial hotline that you can call, or do you need to complete a complicated ritual before you can get connected? The answer is that communicating with your angels is as simple or difficult as you make it!

There will be times when you don't have the time or the inclination to do an hour-long meditation. You need an answer and you need it now! On these occasions you can do the "give it to me" question. Ask the angels a straightforward question in a straightforward way. "Angels, is he attracted to me?" (Angels are telepathic so there is no need to say it out loud, just ask it in your head.) The very first answer that pops into your mind is the correct one. If you want to confirm this, then ask the same question three times, and each time the angels will slip the first answer, "Yes" or "No," into your mind. You may want to argue with it but, even if you do, you will discover its correctness in time. If you have more time, you may wish to consult some angel cards. You can make your own related to love and romance by cutting up some cards and writing on them. "Yes," "No," "Not now," "Wait twenty-four hours," "Go for it," "It will never work out," "Out of your league," etc. When you are stuck for an answer in any given situation, take the cards and ask the angels to guide your hand to the card with the correct message written on it. Again, if you are prone to doubt, repeat the process three times and see how the answers relate to each other.

If you want the full-blown mega-connection with your angels you can do an angel meditation like the one described in Chapter One, with any of the accessories associated with relaxation: Candles, soft music, scent, etc. Spending time in a quiet place with no distractions allows angel messages to float into your mind unhindered. Then again, if angels have something that they want you to know, those messages are just as likely to pop into your head while you are doing housework.

Finally, look out for feathers. These are signs that the angels are trying to tell you something. Naturally don't panic if your feather pillow has a hole in it, but if you find feathers lying around in places where they shouldn't be, know that the angels have something to say to you and give yourself a little peace and quiet to ask them what it is.

Chapter One

You are the One

So you are single ... so what? Okay, so it may feel like everyone else is part of a cozy cuddling couple, but they're not. The world is really made up of just people. Yes, some have coupled up but others are divorced, widowed, between relationships, actively looking, or determinedly unattached. Today's relationships are much more fluid than they used to be so we can all find ourselves single at some point. So, you may be single but (I'm sorry to break this to you) you are not unique.

Archangel Michael

The Warrior

Archangel Michael's name means "He who is like God." His limitless power emanates strength, faith, and courage. His energy aura is a royal blue, so you may find yourself drawn to these colors more when he is around you. You might find deep blue clothes appealing or even see flashes of blue light in front of your eyes. If ever you find yourself in a dangerous situation you can ask Michael to surround you with his protection and you will become invisible to anything that threatens you.

I *think* therefore I'm *single*.   LIZZ WINSTEAD

Being single has always had a bad press. It is synonymous with being a wallflower, "left on the shelf" and missing out on all the fun. This is because the "romance mafia" (from Jane Austen to Barbara Cartland) have brainwashed us into believing that we are no one if we are not one-of-two. But this just doesn't stack up. Some of the most fascinating, intelligent, and attractive people I know are single and this is the least interesting fact about them. Being single is okay. Don't let other people, the media, romantic songs, or any number of sentimental Hollywood films starring John Cusack convince you otherwise.

In the periods in my life when I was single I loved the freedom that it gave me. However, I have also experienced the "downs" of single life. Valentine's Day, Christmas, and vacations can all be difficult. Having a partner brings a shared closeness and understanding as well as passion and romance. Sometimes the responsibility of being alone can be daunting, as it is up to you to make each decision without someone special to bounce thoughts off of. There will be times when you feel empty, challenged, tired, or just fed up. If it all gets too much, you can call in one of the "Big Boys" of the angel world—Archangel Michael.

Michael is one of the best known angels, maybe partly because of John Travolta's depiction of him as a brawling, overweight, cigarette-smoking slob in the 1996 film of the same name. But the real Michael is the essence of love, power, strength, and faith, and if you ask him he will enhance these same qualities in you. You can call on him when

- —You need strength to face something alone.
- —You need to feel safe.
- —You want protection from people or situations.
- —You need a "pick-me-up" to be able to cope.

As they say, "When the going gets tough, the tough get going" and they don't come tougher than Michael, so next time you start to feel that being single is the pits, call on Michael for emotional support and you will be amazed at how much better you start to feel.

As well as Michael you have a guardian angel that never leaves your side. He/she is with you all the time, and always has been. This is a fact, not a myth or a fairy-tale. Nobody on this earth (or beyond) knows you better than your guardian angel does. Every single thing that you have ever experienced—from your first tooth to your first kiss—your guardian angel was right there with you. It may be an unsettling thought to know that your innermost secrets are not secret at all, but this isn't just anybody we are talking about; it's your guardian angel, a being of infinite light and love who can always be trusted to be on your side. Along with the past this wonderful creature also knows all your fears, hopes, and desires for the future; everything that you either dream of or dread.

Julie "I have always had the feeling that there was someone watching over me and directing me. It's an uncanny feeling of having someone or something always next to me."

Angel Advice
things you can do when single

1 Sleep in the "angel position," taking up the whole bed.

2 See any friend anytime (even those of the opposite sex).

3 Wear pajamas/ripped leggings/gray underpants/Kylie T-shirt (insert own fashion faux pas) whenever you want.

4 Be spontaneous.

5 Drive however you want.

6 Control the remote.

7 Not have to shave ... anywhere.

Contacting your
Guardian Angel

Close your eyes and breathe deeply. In your mind's
eye see that you are traveling toward a beautiful
building. It is a temple, with large columns and a
massive golden door. You open the door and find
yourself alone in a room with a high vaulted ceiling.
The sunlight pours in from windows high above your
head. In the middle of the room is a pool so inviting
you walk down the steps into the warm blue water.
The colors of the rainbow reflect back off the water
and light dances around you. All your worries and
cares float away; you feel cleansed and invigorated.

You sense a presence behind you and, in the water's
reflection, you see and know that it is your guardian
angel. You will be aware of whether the spirit is
male or female. Do they have something to tell you?
Open yourself up to the message. Open your mind
and your heart to their overwhelming love. Enjoy
being immersed in the knowledge that you are loved
and cared for on every level.

When you are ready, leave the pool and make your
way to the door. Your guardian angel is behind you,
an ever-present support, guide, and counselor. Open
the great door and close it behind you. Know that
you can return to this wonderful place at any time
that you wish. Slowly, return to the room you are
sitting in and open your eyes.

So, with your newfound guardian angel on your left shoulder and Michael watching your back, being single is more than okay: It is good. Being single is the time when you can really get to know your guardian angel, and yourself. This is the first stage of successful dating; if you don't know who you are, how will anyone else get to know you? Many of us plow on through life ignoring our guardian angel's help and never considering who we really are. How you perceive yourself defines how other people see you, and dating is all about perception. So how do you see yourself? Take a look at yourself in a mirror. Don't just see the familiar face looking back, but really look. If you can't see an angel standing behind you, then you simply aren't looking hard enough.

Moira "About a year ago I went through a particularly lonely period in my life. I had split up with my boyfriend and was living by myself. Everyone else seemed to have someone to care for them; I was alone and depressed. One night I lay in bed and just cried and cried. I got up to go to the bathroom and, as I stood in front of the mirror, I saw an angel behind me. It was at least two feet taller than me, with a white robe, dark shoulder-length hair, and the most amazing green eyes. It placed its arms around me and put its hands over my heart. I knew from that moment that I was never alone. I remember most the feeling of being protected and loved by this being. If ever I feel low or unhappy now I just remember that feeling and I know that I am going to be fine."

Close your eyes again. This time imagine that there is an angel behind you. Don't try too hard to conjure something up, just let an image appear all by itself. This is an impression of your guardian angel. It may be frustratingly fleeting, like catching a glimpse of a friend from a train window, but with practice you will be able to see it in your mind's eye whenever you want.

Not only have I *seen* an angel, I call her my *best friend*. LORI CORKUM

The angels can only help you if you let them. Your guardian angel is ready to send you brilliant messages, but you must be willing to hear them. If you don't open up your mind to receive them it's like trying to watch your favorite program with the television switched off. To encourage angel messages to come into your head, sit quietly, go for a walk, meditate, or do some exercise, anything that helps you to declutter your thoughts. I go swimming, because in the water I can let my mind float as well as my body. It helps to avoid electronic equipment; televisions, radios, stereos, computers, and playstations all seem to interfere with the reception of angel messages. You can't hear an angel whispering if you have your iPod in both ears.

A very simple way to connect is just to acknowledge your guardian angel mentally and ask for help. It's as easy as that. If you wake up each morning and say, "Hi, guardian angel, please be with me today to help and guide me" you will immediately notice the difference in your life. This also applies to your love life because your guardian angel can change the way that you date and relate to other people. The first thing your guardian angel can do is help you to understand yourself better. This only works if you are willing to be honest, and I do mean completely honest, as there is no point in trying to pull the wool over your guardian angel's eyes. If you are prepared to be completely truthful, you can start the process of finding out who you are and what you like; then you can find someone who likes what you like and who likes you. Couples who like the same things and share the same beliefs are more likely to stay together. So if you love sushi, shopping, and Shakespeare and you unexpectedly happen to meet a rich Japanese actor, the chances are that you will get on famously.

Once you know what you really like and what is really important to you, begin to fill your life with these things. If you like cats, own one. If your family matters to you, spend time with them. If your career is high on your list, work hard to succeed at it. Make conscious decisions so that your outer life reflects your inner self.

Who are you?

Go somewhere quiet where you can think clearly and you won't be disturbed. Take a pen and paper and jot the numbers 1–10 down the side of the page. That much I am sure you can do without angel help, but now I want you to ask your guardian angel to tell you ten things that you really like. Don't think about it too hard or censor anything that comes through, just write down the first ten things that pop into your head. It doesn't matter if some of them seem trivial or unimportant—put them on your list anyway. Also, don't worry if you can't think of ten, or that you come up with fifteen—the number of items is not important, the message is. This may seem a basic thing to do, but bear with me (and the angels) as we are going somewhere with this.

Next, jot the numbers 1–10 down again and this time next to each number write down something that is really important to you. Again, don't stop to consider each item, just let your guardian angel reveal the answers to you. You may be amazed by what ends up on the page. Remember, there are no right or wrong answers. You might be tempted to adjust your answers but there's absolutely no point as you will only be cheating yourself—your guardian angel knows what you should have written anyway. Keep this list safe, as we will come back to it in the next chapter.

Some people might argue that filling your life with a lot of things makes you too busy to find love, but the opposite is true. The more that you establish a fun-filled, fulfilling life, the more you will attract the right person. There is a universal law that says that energy attracts similar energy, so if you want someone who is fascinating and fun, you must first become fascinating and fun yourself. If you don't want someone who is boringly tedious, then why should anyone want you if you are a tedious bore? Once you have created a life for yourself, a lover will then be a delicious addition to it, and not the only thing on the list.

Projecting the real you out to the universe is a great start to successful dating. One of the biggest problems with dating is the falseness: So often people pretend to be someone they are not. This is understandable because everyone is out to impress, but exaggeration will only lead to aggravation. A little fib can grow into a big lie and dishonesty is the worst possible foundation for a relationship. So if you pretend to be wealthier, healthier, smarter or better connected than you really are, you will get caught out. If you want other people to be honest with you, you must be honest with them. Angels only know honesty and if you ask for their help they will give you the courage to be totally true to yourself.

One great thing you can do better when you are single than at any other time in your life is invest in your friends. Friends are fabulous and they can sustain you through the most desolate of times. However, friends don't just happen, they need to be cultivated. The definition of "cultivation" is "to cherish, to foster, to improve by labor." It takes hard work to grow healthy, mature friendships but you can be sure that no act of friendship, however small, is ever wasted. If you take the time and put the effort in you will reap the rewards of real friendship; and the best time to do this is when you are single. This is simply because you

There is a *magnet* in your heart that will attract *true friends*. PARAMAHANSA YOGANANDA will have more time available. When you are dating, a lot of your social time will be taken up with potential lovers, so use your single time to see friends, spend time with them, and really get to know them. You will never regret that you did. They say that you can count your true friends on one hand. Well, I never bother putting a number on my true friends. People are in your life for a reason, a season, or forever; you will find that some friends come and go with no recriminations while others hang around until you all check into the nursing home together. None is more valuable than any other. However, just imagine for a moment that you wake up and find yourself naked in the middle of Grand Central Station with nothing but a cell phone. Who do you call? These people are your friends.

Angels are constantly influencing us to make friends and improve relationships with other people because this is how we learn about others and ourselves. Your guardian angel is in constant contact with many other people's guardian angels. It's a bit like a celestial chat room that goes on in the ether without us ever knowing about it. That is why those "spooky" coincidences happen when you are just thinking of someone and the next minute you bump into them in the street, or someone you haven't thought of for ages pops into your mind and a second later they phone you up. Your guardian angel is talking to their guardian angel and they are both passing the message on. Imagine how useful this can be when it comes to dating.

Angel Advice
things being single IS NOT

1 A waiting room.

2 Unusual: Over twenty million Americans live alone—that's a quarter of the nation's households.

3 A justification for wearing corduroy.

4 A reason to sleep with just anyone.

5 Compulsory: You can always find someone to share a pizza with.

6 An excuse to feel sorry for yourself.

7 Being alone: It is being by yourself, which is different.

Melanie "My first husband and I had just broken up after a very stormy marriage. We'd had the final row and he'd left. At the time, my best friend was staying in Germany, but she came home unexpectedly. Normally she would phone me a day or two after she got back, but that night, the night my husband left, she got in from the airport at midnight, and felt she 'just had to' phone me. She didn't know why, but it was a very strong conviction that she needed to speak to me. (This was in the days before cell phones.)"

It's unlikely that you will be single forever, so enjoy this time. It is not easy to relax into ambiguity, but the more that you do so the happier you will be. When the timing is right you will be busy dating so make the most of your single time.

If you treat yourself to something, you will feel better about everything. Certain angels are assigned to help you to spoil yourself. Call them the **Naughty Angels** *if you like. They will prompt you to do something selfish and not feel bad about it afterward. Have you ever spontaneously bought something wildly expensive or done something recklessly foolish but fun? If you now own that fake fur coat, or still have the scars from that skydive, then you have been influenced by the* **Naughty Angels**.

Now you are willing to celebrate your single status. You are neither a loser nor a social leper; you are a valued and valuable human being. The angels will keep reminding you of that. Your single time is the time to get to know yourself, get to know your friends, and get to know your guardian angel. When you are happy with yourself and the life you have created, and have a solid foundation of support from angels, friends, and/or family—that is the time to start dating.

The most *profound* relationship we will ever have is the one with *ourselves*.   SHIRLEY MACLAINE

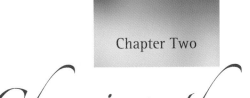

Chapter Two

Choosing the One

So, are you ready to take the plunge and start dating? Maybe you would rather dip your toe into the dating pool first? Maybe you have already been for a swim and found the water too choppy, so you are worried about being swept away? Perhaps you have just come out of a long-term relationship or a marriage and you are wary of getting wet at all. Whatever your situation, the angels will keep you afloat and Raphael is the angel to see you safely onto dry land.

Archangel Raphael

The Friend

Raphael gives you guidance through intuition, ideas, or dreams. The way he works is by slipping thoughts into your mind when you are least expecting them. If you have ever had a brilliant idea and wondered why you hadn't thought of it before, or if you have woken up one morning and suddenly everything made sense, then you have been visited by Raphael. His aura shows as an emerald green energy so you may be attracted to this color when he is helping you.

Angel Advice

signs that you are
ready to start dating

1 You send yourself
a Valentine's card
(again).

2 You want to tell
someone that great
joke you just heard.

3 You are happy to
eat beans every night.

4 Even your friends
hang up on you.

5 You watch the
Hallmark Channel
24/7.

6 You French-kiss the
pillow.

7 The owner of the
DVD rental store
sends you a birthday
card.

Raphael is another one of the seven Archangels so he is pretty powerful but he is also considered to be the chattiest and friendliest of the angels. He is like a good buddy, and if you can't be honest with a good buddy, then who can you be honest with? And I do need you to be honest here. If I needed honesty from you in Chapter One, I need it in truckloads now. Remember the importance of honesty and how it all begins with you.

If you ask for Raphael's help he will enable you to understand more clearly what kind of partner you want in your life. You may already think you know exactly what sort of lover you desire: Perhaps they must be intelligent, gorgeous, and stinking rich before they even warrant a glance. I know a girl who will only consider a man if he drives a convertible, lives on a ranch, and owns a yacht. She is still single. Maybe it is time for her (and you) to reassess what you really want from a partner—with some help from Raphael.

Before you do this, there is one word that you must remove from your vocabulary and that word is "should." "I should have a partner," "I should be married by the time I'm thirty," "They should have a Ferrari." The word "should" comes from having expectations of people and things. Occasionally expectations are reasonable (it's okay to expect a date not to smell of cabbage or burp loudly when they shake your hand), but other expectations can be so rigid that they can stop you from dating before you've even begun. Sometimes it's hard to know where our expectations come from. They can be thrust upon us by others, stuck on us by the media, or created all by ourselves from past experiences. The girl I just mentioned is a good example. She comes from a fairly wealthy family and she admits that her greatest fear is disappointing her mother. She thinks that if she took a penniless man home to meet the family her mother would hit the roof. I pointed out to her that her mother had already met her partner for life (when, incidentally they were both poor students) so why did she care the slightest bit what her mother thought? Living up to other people's expectations can narrow your potential for finding someone who will make you happy, so come on—at least give them a chance.

When you decide what you want in a partner do not be vague or fluffy. You can't just say, "I want someone who will make me happy." That's too fluffy. In order for the right partner to come into your life you must define what the right partner means to you. This means drawing up a list of qualities that you wish your partner to possess, in other words defining what you really want instead of what you think you want.

Love has nothing to do with what you are expecting to *get*—only with what you are expecting to *give*—which is *everything*.

KATHARINE HEPBURN

What do you want?

You are about to make another list, so get the pen and do the numbers from 1–10 again. This time ask Archangel Raphael to guide you as you list the things that you want from a partner. You may find the most unusual characteristics popping into your mind, from the ubiquitous "good sense of humor" to size eleven feet. Write whatever pops into your mind, even if the features are strange or embarrassing or they reveal aspects of your own personality that you would rather keep hidden. If it is important to you that a partner has a bulging bank account, then you must add "wealthy" to the list. No one but you (and Raphael) is going to know about this list, so be brutally honest. You may have some curious characteristics that you consider to be vital in a partner, like "brilliant bassoon player" or "New York Yankees supporter" and that is exactly as it should be. Everyone is different, so each list will be different.

Now, if we go back to your two lists from Chapter One, you have established a set of beliefs and values that define who you are. If you are confident and proud that these criteria sum you up, we can now see how they apply to a potential partner. It is time to put all three lists together to form a picture of someone who will be perfect for you.

Begin with the last list first and work backward, writing down all the important qualities that your partner must possess. You will find that some traits appear in more than one list so your final list of personality characteristics will probably be less than thirty (most are around twenty). This is your own personal Raphael List and it is a very useful little weapon to have in your dating armory. From now on, you can measure anyone that you meet against this list. You will be looking for them to score highly in the top categories, then as you go down the list you will be more flexible.

Let's say that being close to your family is really important to you and it is right up there at number 1. It is not going to work if you date someone who couldn't care less about his/her family and can't understand why yours matters so much to you. If you are a fitness fanatic and have "physically fit" at number 2, then dating a couch potato will prove difficult. If you love animals, then dating someone who goes deer hunting will bring problems. I'm sure you get my drift. Somewhere around about number 15 you will be able to tolerate a degree of difference.

Angel Advice

things not to expect from a partner

1 Telepathy—only the angels can do this.

2 Matching underwear.

3 Fluent Swahili (unless you live in East Africa).

4 Complete honesty (at least at first—see Jophiel's Three Date Policy, Chapter Five).

5 Bank account details.

6 Kama Sutra sex.

7 Perfection—again this belongs only to the angels.

Now that you have created a detailed description of the kind of person you really want, you may find that they are very different from the person you originally thought that you wanted. In my friend's completed list there was no mention of a convertible, a ranch, or a yacht.

Try to date someone who likes what you like, agrees with what you think is important, and, wants what you want from life. In other words, try to date someone who is a lot like you. Like I said in Chapter One, there is a universal law stating that energy attracts similar energy, so if you project who you really are out to the world, someone similar will be drawn to you. This is angel magic.

It is important to be very specific and include everything on your Raphael List, as leaving out anything, even the simplest thing that seems inconsequential to you at the time, can have unexpected repercussions. This was clearly demonstrated to me by a lady who told me a cautionary tale. She had carefully listed the qualities that she desired in her ideal man and used this in combination with her own lists of her likes and what is important to her to form her complete Raphael List. She then duly asked the angels to bring her a man who embodied all the elements of the list. Not long after, sure enough, she met a man who ticked all her boxes. She was bowled over by him as he personified every single trait that she had requested. There was just one problem—he was already married. She had omitted the fact that he should be single from her list. Talk about disappointment. So please make absolutely sure every characteristic that you need is on your list.

Raphael will replace your expectations with intentions. What's the difference between the two? Well, if you *expect* something, you will, more often than not, be disappointed. However, if you *intend* something, then you can make sure that you are never disappointed. (Of course, there is the odd occasion when you expect something bad and you are pleasantly surprised, but this doesn't happen very often.) Other people control whether your expectations will be fulfilled or not, but only you control your own intentions. For example, looking back at my own life, I expected to be married by the time that I was thirty. Because I was with someone who did not want to marry me, I hit the big "Three O" without a wedding ring on my finger. However, I always intended to be a wife and I fulfilled that intention when I was thirty-six by being with someone who did want to marry me.

Our *intention* creates our *reality*.

WAYNE DYER

Emma "The first time I went on a date with Steven I decided that he was the man for me. I can't explain why or what it was about him, but I knew I wanted to spend the rest of my life with him. By the end of 1999 we had been together three years and I was absolutely convinced that he was going to propose on Millennium Night. We were on vacation in Australia and I had got all dressed up for the occasion. As we sipped champagne under the stars I waited for him to pop the question but ... nothing, just a Happy New Year kiss. I was devastated. I had been so sure that he would do it—I mean, I had dropped enough hints.

Anyway, I realized that I had been stupid to get my hopes up so I just accepted that being with him was more important than any wedding ring. Two weeks later, back home, while we were walking in the woods near our house, he asked me to marry him. He said that he had felt under pressure to 'get it right' in Australia so it didn't feel right but here where we are so happy he knew it was what he wanted."

Emma's expectations of Steven made him uncomfortable and left her disappointed. Her acceptance of her intention to stay with him, no matter what, freed her from those expectations and made her happy. This clearly shows the difference between expectation and intention, and why intention is so much more powerful and positive than expectation. The very act of accepting that something may never happen is often what can bring it about. It may be very difficult for a potential partner to live up to your rigid expectations of

I *knew* I loved you before I met you.

SAVAGE GARDEN

them, but they may well be able to fit into your intentions. Intentions are flexible and can change depending on the situation. Replace "I should have a partner" with "I intend to have a partner at some point." Replace "I should be married by the time I'm thirty" with "I intend to get married when I meet the right person." Instead of "They should have a Ferrari" try "They may have a Ferrari." Intentions take the pressure off and replace it with possibilities. Intentions can help you to widen your potential to find someone who will make you really happy.

Angels can help you to set positive, achievable intentions which they help you to fulfill. They are brilliant celestial life coaches. However, in losing your expectations and replacing them with intentions do not slip down the slippery slope into the wimpy world of "hope." You are not "hoping" to meet someone; you "intend" to meet someone. You are in control of this process.

Once you have an accurate idea of your partner-to-be, you can begin to visualize them. Remember that Raphael puts ideas, thoughts, and pictures into your mind's eye, so if you ask him he can place an image of your future partner in your mind. Don't forget that (unless they are very much younger than you) your future lover already exists somewhere on the planet, so it is easy for Raphael to conjure up how they look. You will begin to sense whether they are tall or small, dark or fair,

Angel Advice
reasons to visualize your partner

1 You will recognize them when you meet them.

2 It beats watching television.

3 It keeps the energy of your intention high.

4 It brings them to you quicker.

5 "Seeing is believing," so if you see them you can believe in them.

6 They are a delight to look at.

7 You can astound your friends later with your powers of prediction.

rounded or slender. You can then refine this picture until it is perfectly clear in your head, then you can begin to relate to it. See them laughing, walking, talking, eating, and even kissing you. You may even have a very vivid dream in which they feature. This is not as weird as it sounds. You can trust Raphael—he is your friend.

Your "imaginary" boy/girlfriend is not really imaginary at all. When you visualize them you experience a premonition of meeting them and this very act brings them closer to you. This is because everything is made up of energy and we are nothing more than bundles of neutrons and electrons bouncing around. The angels are also energy, but they operate on a higher frequency than we do so they bounce around much more quickly than us. That is why we can't (usually) see them. Just as there are sound waves or light waves that we cannot hear or see, there are angel waves that are all around us. When you visualize someone you tap into these angel waves (like switching on your receiver) and you are able to download the image that the angels send you. That is why some people experience the phenomenon of love at first sight. The angels have shown them their future love, so when they actually see them in person they get a sense of déjà vu. (See Jophiel's "Wow!" factor in Chapter Five.)

The *best* mirror is an *old friend*.

GEORGE HERBERT

Thomas "I always knew what my wife would look like even before I met her. I knew she would be blonde and tall and I even knew that she would have a certain way of walking. I even used to dream of this girl. One day I was driving in the pouring rain and I turned at a crossroads and nearly ran over her. I swear it was the scariest thing that has ever happened to me. There she was, the girl I had only ever imagined. She was pushing a stroller, so I figured that she was married. Just my luck; meet the girl of my dreams and she's not available. Three years later we met again when she was going through a divorce and you can guess the rest. I have never told her or anyone else about this before because it was just all too freaky."

If you visualize your future partner often you will create an unstoppable force of energy that brings them to you. Once you create an intention and visualize it you begin a process of attracting that very thing into your life. It becomes a self-fulfilling prophecy.

So, now that you have a detailed idea of your partner-to-be, you can ask the angels to bring this person into your life. But be sure to do it in the right way. Even the actual words that you use are important. Angels will literally take you at your word. For example, if you say, "I want a partner," they will simply give you the "wanting." If you say, "I need to find a partner," you will be left with the "needing." I know it sounds odd, but there seems to be something lost in translation and unless you ask in the right way, you may not get the result that you intend. The way to ask the angels to bring your partner to you is to say:

- "I am ready for a partner to come into my life" or
- "I am willing to allow a partner into my life" or
- "I am ready to receive a partner in my life."

Any of those three will do the trick, and if you don't believe me just go ahead and try them out.

Val "My friend Julia was always convinced that she would marry a man with a gold tooth. Every time she met a new man she would discreetly check out his teeth as she was talking to him. Of course most of them didn't have a gold tooth in their head so they were rejected without ever really knowing why. In the end she agreed with me that basing a whole relationship on a gold tooth was a bit ridiculous. Not long afterward, she met her husband at a cricket club dinner. He had a full head of teeth but she fell in love with him anyway. Now this is where things get strange, because six years after they were married (and she had forgotten all about the gold tooth) he got hit in the face with a cricket ball and lost two teeth. He decided that he would replace them with gold crowns. I used to tell Julia that she had wasted so much time looking for her gold-toothed hero, but now I wonder if she was meant to wait until she found the right man."

You now know who you are as well as who you want, you have asked the angels to bring this person into your life, and you are working with the energy of the universe in order to bring this about. With your Raphael List tucked into your pocket you are ready to dip your toe, go wading or dive right into the dating pool. So let's go dating ...

Finding the One

You now know beyond doubt that you want a George Clooney/Angelina Jolie look-alike with size eleven feet who plays the bassoon, supports the New York Yankees, is kind to animals, and has a healthy bank account. That's the easy part. Now for the hard part—finding them. This requires the matchmaking services of a very powerful angel, the Archangel Gabriel. She oversees every form of communication in the universe so if you need to find anyone, ask Gabriel to do the hard work. She will guide you to the love of your life through thoughts, feelings, and intuition.

The Messenger

Gabriel is a feminine energy, which makes
sense as some people would say that women
communicate better than men. Her name means
"Messenger of God" so she is often depicted with
a trumpet, signifying her role as an important
messenger. If all the angels are messengers, then
she is the postmistress. Her energy works through
a pure white color so you may have an affinity
with this color when she is helping you.

Archangel Gabriel

I *know* that somewhere in the *Universe* exists my *perfect soul mate*–but looking for her is much more *difficult* than just staying at home and ordering another pizza. ALF WHIT

When Gabriel is with you, you may get an urge to go to a party or a park, visit a friend, join a club or go to a café. You may have a sudden impulse to go walking, shopping, jogging, or bungee jumping. Something in a newspaper may catch your eye; a radio or television show may give you an idea; I have even known computers to log onto websites of their own accord and text messages to be redirected to different people. Be open to Gabriel's messages as she nudges you toward romance with her wings. You will find that things happen naturally and potential partners appear from nowhere.

Charli "I had been divorced exactly a week and although I was ready to accept my life as a single mom and I had a lot to be thankful for, I hoped that I would meet someone else. I decided to redecorate the house so I looked in a local newspaper for a decorator. When he knocked on the door it was instant attraction, like 'Oh, there you are.' We have been together two years now and I still say that the angels brought him to me when I was ready. I thank them for that every day."

I know that Charli is very much in touch with the angels and that she always acts instinctively on their messages. One of those messages was the idea to decorate her house; the next was that particular phone number which jumped off the page at her, but she still had to pick up the phone and dial. Gabriel will do the hard work, but you have to make an effort yourself. If you slob on the sofa whining about the fact that all the good ones are married or gay, then you've only got yourself to blame—and you can be sure that Gabriel is behind you flapping her wings. Most people put more time, effort, and thought into buying a new car than they do finding a lover. This is crazy because a new car will always deteriorate in value while a lover may become the most precious thing in your life.

Many people looking for love get hung up on the "when" of it all: When will I meet someone, when will I fall in love, when will I get married? This is partly due to the pressure that society puts on us to conform to certain "norms"; you should be dating in your teens, serious about someone in your twenties, married by your thirties, and so on. (You will notice the word "should" is back again in all of these "norms.") I remember one man who came to see me while he was going through a painful divorce at the age of twenty-nine. He said, "I wish someone had told me that there was plenty of time." Ask yourself which is preferable: buying the first used car you come across, which could break down, or taking your time and finding your dream car?

It is important to know that everything happens in divine timing. If you have asked the angels to bring you a lover, and you are willing to listen to their guidance, then a lover will come to you. You must believe that this will happen. Doubting will only slow the whole process down. Instead of focusing on the "when" it will happen, concentrate on the "how."

There are so many ways to find a partner: singles bars, personal columns, speed dating, dinners, clubs, and vacations. (By the way, don't pay any attention to anyone who turns their nose up at any of these methods—they probably met their partner at grade school and secretly feel that they are missing out.) There is also the all-powerful internet. Fifty million people have used internet dating sites and while some of the users may indeed be complete fruitcakes, that still leaves over forty million who are nice, normal people just wanting to find love. They use the world wide web because they are too busy, too shy, or too

Help *yourself* and heaven will help *you*.

JEAN DE LA FONTAINE

exhausted to search any other way ... and why not? It's safe, it's quick, it's warm, and it's a great way to narrow down your search. The internet creates connections that would not (could not) happen in any other way. How else could you meet a plumber from Peru while you're sitting in your pajamas in Pittsburgh?

Jenny "I used to date a guy who went back to live on the East Coast. We were pretty serious about each other but we were young and when he left we lost touch. Years went by and I had several long-term relationships, but for some reason I never forgot him. I found myself single again last year and decided to try to look him up and see how his life had gone. I figured he would be married with kids but I just wanted to let him know that I still thought about him. I searched for him on the net and got nowhere. I only had his name and the state he had moved back to. I didn't know if he still lived there.

I must have tried at least four times to get in touch with him and I was about to give up when I had one last try. To my amazement he responded. He had only decided to go online that day and he doesn't know what made him do so; it was as if someone or something had prompted him to do it. It was an amazing experience, contacting him after all these years. He had been married but was now divorced and when I went to visit him at Christmas it was as if we had never been apart."

Gabriel is the angel who oversees the internet. Angels love anything that is made up of energy and they will play with radios, light bulbs—anything electrical. They particularly love computers. Take a minute before you log on to the internet to ask Archangel Gabriel to guide you through the world wide web and you will be amazed. You will find surfing becomes a breeze. You will find the right site, the right words, and the right person, as the angels will be manipulating energy in the ether to make it happen.

You only have to ask for Gabriel to get involved and you will be amazed at how much easier it becomes to meet potential mates. And there is more good news. There is no such thing as a soul mate. I know that some people hope to meet "the one" person out there who is their other half. But you are not half a person. Look at it logically. If there was just one person on this planet that was meant for you and you alone, what are the odds that you would bump into them at the right time and the right place? It's a big world and they might live in Acapulco while you live in Arkansas. Even with Gabriel busting a gut to make it happen, I don't care for the odds on you finding just one person to love in a population of 6.6 billion. You've got more chance of winning the lottery and you haven't hit the jackpot yet, have you?

The idea of a soul mate is a myth and it is very sad when people throw away a potentially good relationship because it doesn't shape up to a fictional image of what their soul mate "should" be like. It's a bit like turning down George Clooney because he is not Mr Incredible or Angelina Jolie because she is not Jessica Rabbit. Do not get hung up on the idea that you must seek out your one and

Angel Advice
good chat-up lines

1 "I have a Swiss bank account."

2 "Fat penguin"—it always breaks the ice.

3 "Can I buy you a drink or do you just want the money?"

4 "If I asked you out would your answer be the same as the answer to this question?"

5 "Can I buy you a car with that drink?"

6 "I bet ten bucks you'll turn me down."

7 "I'm not very good at chat-up lines."

Angel Advice
bad chat-up lines

1 "I didn't believe in angels till I met you."

2 "Let's go and do all the things that I'll tell everyone we did anyway."

3 "You're ugly but I'm intrigued."

4 "Hi, my friends call me weird."

5 "You look great from behind."

6 "Cheer up, personality is important too."

7 "You'll do."

only "soul mate" at all costs. You will be wasting your time. They simply don't exist. Instead there are many possible soul mates, all of whom could score highly on your Raphael List. This should come as very good news to you. We have just increased your dating odds from one to who-knows-how-many? Things are looking up already.

The next piece of good news from Gabriel is that no one is perfect. Again, this meets with a mixed reaction because some people are expecting to meet someone who is perfection personified. They will be disappointed. Let go of the concept of the perfect man or the perfect woman and you free yourself from years of disillusion and disappointment. Instead of endlessly searching for someone who is perfect, look for someone who is perfect for you, someone whom you deserve and who deserves you.

No matter how it happens, with Gabriel on your side you will meet someone who is a possible love match. In fact, sometimes Gabriel is a little too powerful and once you ask for her help you may find that you are in the "bus scenario." After a dating drought there is a sudden deluge and several potentials arrive at the same time. No matter how tempting it may be, do not fall into the trap of keeping your options open. Even if three gorgeous, fantastic, loaded people all turn up at once, choose just one of them to invest in. (If you can't decide, then ask Gabriel which is the right one and she will tell you.) If you keep half a mind on the other two you are setting the intention that the first one will not succeed. Planning what to wear on Saturday night means Friday night will be a disaster.

Once Gabriel has found you someone, you can ask for her help to plan the first date (if it's down to you to do it). You will receive a good idea out of the blue. Instead of the unimaginative "dinner and a club" Gabriel can suggest somewhere to make the occasion particularly memorable. The first date should ideally be in daylight and outdoors. There are obvious safety advantages in this, but a lesser-known benefit is that angels can communicate with you more easily in the open air. It is also easier for you to communicate with the other person. Going to see a movie may be a traditional choice but you are unlikely to discover much about your date except that they like Johnny Depp or Keira Knightley. Instead, go to a park, a market, for a picnic, to the races, or to the countryside. If you go somewhere that has an element of adventure to it, not only will you impress them with your originality but they will also associate you with feeling excited and elated, which is no bad thing. Naturally don't be tempted to take this adventurous stuff too far and book a parachute jump, as they may suffer from vertigo. Your choice of date says things about you, too, so if you want to appear interesting and fun, then pick a date idea that reflects this.

Successful dating requires honesty on both sides. One girl who came to see me viewed dating as a war zone. She expected each man she met to be a liar and a cheat so she was just waiting to catch the poor guy out and say, "Aha, I'm right, you are a bastard." Consequently, she always came across as cautious and cold. I told her that she could change the way that she looked at men if she used angel eyes. If she saw each new date as innocent until proven guilty she would have a

If you would be *loved*, love and be *lovable*.

BENJAMIN FRANKLIN

completely different dating experience. Months later she came to me again and the change in her was profound. She was in touch with her angels, she was enjoying her life enormously, and she sparkled with joy and fun. She was also in the process of (seriously) dating a very nice man. She told me that the minute she began to look for honesty instead of deceit she was able to open up and trust. If you expect to be lied to, hurt, and messed around before you even leave the house, then you make these things more likely to happen. Remember that universal law of energy attracting similar energy. If you want truth, kindness, and honesty to come your way you must first project it to others.

Most people fall into one of two categories: "radiators" or "drains." "Radiators" are the people who act instinctively on the angel messages that they are sent. They tend to think the best of others, do small acts of kindness, and generally spread a little happiness. You probably know a few "radiators," and you probably really like them.

"Drains" are just the opposite. They ignore any kind of angel communication and they think that everyone is out to mess them around and tell everyone else about it. "Drains" are people who are afraid. They are afraid of being hurt, looking silly, getting embarrassed, being talked about, being run over by a ten-ton truck, and a thousand other things. They let fear rule their lives and, because it has got them in a vice-like grip, they like to spread it around and let it grab other people too. You probably also have a "drain" somewhere in your life and you may do your best to avoid them.

Dating is so much easier if you try to be a "radiator" rather than a "drain."

Davina "I met a man on a blind date and we commiserated about our dead parents. He had lost his mother; I had lost my father. We were both near tears several times. He was a wonderfully nice guy, but I think we were both just too depressing for each other."

Most people in the world are not mad, bad, or dangerous to know, they are just doing their best. Giving them the benefit of the doubt means that they can be their best too.

The age-old question of what to wear on a first date is answered by the **Fashion Angels**. *They can help you to select just the right outfit so that you feel confident and comfortable. As a rule of thumb they will usually guide you to clothes that you normally wear. Obviously they won't highlight jogging bottoms or old decorating dungarees, but they will direct you to an outfit that you have always felt relaxed wearing. If you have ever spent a fortune on a new dress/suit for a date only to leave it lying on the bed while you go out in your favorite jeans, you have been influenced by the* **Fashion Angels**. *The same applies to makeup and hair. If you spend three hours at the hairdresser's before going on a date, then you will give a false impression of what you usually look like. This may not seem important, but it all adds up to approaching the date with as much honesty as possible, and this includes being honest about how you look.*

Angel Advice
places not to go on a first date

1 A sex shop.

2 A swingers' party.

3 Your friend's house.

4 A slaughterhouse.

5 An STD clinic.

6 A funeral.

7 Your ex's house.

Gabriel can help you to find someone to date, choose where to go, decide what to wear, and be yourself. You are almost ready to go, but there is one last thing to consider before you call the taxi, and again I need you to be honest. Are you expecting certain things to happen? Maybe you expect the sun to shine, the conversation to sparkle, and the sexual chemistry to sizzle. The chances are that one of these factors will not measure up, in which case you will be left feeling dissatisfied, so leave your human expectations at home and take angelic intentions with you instead. Tell yourself that you intend to have fun, no matter what happens. Then, even if it rains, you have nothing to say to each other, and you don't find them the tiniest bit attractive, you will still feel happy. Don't forget: You are in control of your intentions and how you feel—nothing and no one else can influence that. Okay, so now you are finally ready to go on a date, with the angels helping you all the way.

Chapter Four

Meeting the One

Setting off on a first date can be terrifying, especially if you consider all the things that could happen. Your date might turn out to be awful, boring, and ugly. Then again they may be gorgeous, sexy, funny, and brilliant—then you really are in trouble. If you stopped to think about all the potential pitfalls (from spilled wine to sloppy kissing) you would never go. So don't bother. Instead, let the angels do the worrying for you. The best angel to help you out on a first date is Archangel Uriel.

Archangel Uriel

The Thinker

Uriel means "Light of God" and his role is to spread light around the world. If you ask him, he can shower his luminosity on you so that you radiate with an inner glow. His energy is a pale yellow color like a candle glow, so you may even feel more light and warmth around you.

Just the very act of telling Uriel your concerns about the date will make you more relaxed, but there are other ways that he can help, too. His great ability is to illuminate people and situations, so if you ask him he will make you sparkle like a diamond. He can make things brighter all around you. If you are meeting someone and you don't know what they look like, ask Uriel to point them out to you and they will literally stand out in a crowd. If you are going to a restaurant, one table will call to you and this will be the best one for you to sit at. If the waiter hands you the wine list, ask Uriel which one to choose and one name will seem to be written in larger letters than the others. Uriel's messages jump into your head and make even the most confusing situations seem simple.

Hanna "The worst first date I ever had was with a guy who was so nervous that he kept 'discreetly' looking down at his lap at questions that he had written to ask me. This might have been cute, except that he didn't listen to my answer before sneaking a peek at the next question. When the dinner was over and we got up to go, the cards spilled all over the floor. I suppose it was a good idea gone wrong."

One group of angels oversees the art of flirting. If you call upon their help they will turn you into an incredible flirt. You will suddenly no longer be in control of your body as it employs every trick in the book to attract its prey: You will glance enticingly and look away at just the right instant; then you will begin to hold eye contact for an indecent amount of time; your pupils will dilate as you instinctively play with your hair and move your body into various inviting positions; your voice tone will drop to a seductive growl as you say all the right things. Before you know it, you are lightly touching hands and stroking skin. The **Flirting Angels** *are very playful and they encourage you to be the same, so don't resist.*

One of the best things that Uriel can do for you is boost your confidence. It is so much easier to be confident when even the wine list is on your side. However, there is a fine line between confidence and cockiness. To show off is

Honesty is the cornerstone of all *success*.

MARY KAY ASH

to put off, so Uriel will make you self-assured but not self-obsessed. After all, a conversation is not a competition. You will not be awarded points by a secret panel judging how clever, witty, or erudite you are. Then again there is no need to be humble and play down your attributes either. If you ask for Uriel's help he will give you the confidence to be honest. You will be that most elusive of things on a date—yourself.

Diane "A few years ago, I was working in an insurance office and a really good-looking man who also worked there asked me to meet him for a coffee break. I was thrilled beyond words, as he was so cute in every way. As he sauntered off to the elevator where I was waiting, I quipped, 'Hurry up, you act like you have a wooden leg,' to which he replied, 'I do.'"

Total honesty is not always the best policy on a first date. You may have had the experience of blurting out something and regretting it later. If you have just shaken hands with someone, it's probably not a great idea to say, "Oh, you're gorgeous, I want to see you naked." If you are afraid of saying the wrong thing, you can use Uriel's speech monitor, which will insure that only the right words come out of your mouth. Simply ask Uriel to guide what you say; you will find that not only does the conversation flow effortlessly but also you won't put your proverbial foot in it. In the same way, Uriel will also prevent you from revealing too much, too soon. It's one thing not to lie, but it's another to give away intimate details when you've hardly met. "Hello, I bite my nails, hate Brussels sprouts, fantasize about having a threesome, and once stole a bath towel from a hotel" might be too much information to throw at someone right away and may scare them off. Discretion is the angelic part of honesty.

Angel Advice
first-date do's

1 Be punctual.

2 Smile.

3 Compliment your date.

4 Take enough money with you.

5 Be polite, say thank you, and have fun.

6 Flirt with your date.

7 Talk about things you know about and are interested in.

Just being yourself is really hard on a first date. Bear in mind also that not everyone is what they first appear to be. Some people believe that lying will get them what they want more easily and quickly. If you discover this about them early on, you can avoid heartache later. This is where Uriel's power of enlightenment is invaluable. He can give you the detachment to see the other person clearly. It is so easy to be blinded by good looks and charm, especially when your heart is hungry and you are willing them to be what you want them to be. However, what you see (or hear) is not always what you get. Remember that truth is the first casualty when people are out to impress each other. This leads to a mutual fantasy world where they say fictional things and you endorse what they say—in other words, they lie and you believe them.

—"Last week I took the jet over to Monte Carlo and did a parachute jump for charity."
—"Wow, really, did you break anything?"
—"Only the world record for a successful free fall."

When you have only just met someone it can be difficult to separate reality from fantasy. They may really have a jet and go parachuting. Of course some lies are easier to detect than others.—a 300-pound guy is not likely to be a champion jockey and a tiny girl probably isn't a catwalk model—but some fibs are more difficult to detect. If someone claims to be honest, faithful, wealthy, and kind, how do you know whether they are or not?

If you want to know when someone is lying to you, you can use **Uriel's lie detector** *(or B.S. detector). All you need to do is ask Uriel to give you a sign whenever the other person tells a lie. You choose what the sign is, but make sure that it is a recognizable physical sign that you cannot dismiss. Maybe you can ask that your foot taps on the floor, your tongue tingles, or your leg twitches. You will probably forget all about it until the other person tells a fib, at which point I guarantee you will feel the sign.*

My favorite story about Uriel's lie detector was from a friend of mine, who asked that her bra strap should twang each time someone lied to her. Unfortunately she went on a date with a compulsive liar and by the end of the evening she had developed a nervous twitch and her shoulder was turning black and blue. So, a word of warning: Do not ask Uriel to make your eyes blink, your nose wrinkle, or your tongue stick out or you may end up frightening everyone within a half-mile radius.

Uriel will reveal things to you about the other person by steering the conversation in certain directions. Think of him as an invisible conductor, orchestrating the events of the date in order to provide you with the most information possible. He will place thoughts in your head that help you to ask the right questions and talk about appropriate subjects. Instead of coming right out with, "So, are you faithful or do you mess around?" (direct but not very subtle), he will guide you to tell a story that involves some kind of loyalty; maybe a friend stuck by you in a difficult situation, or you worked extra hours to help your boss. Whatever the story, watch how your date reacts to it. Do they approve of the self-sacrifice or do they make fun of it? That is how you know what loyalty means to them.

It is better to trust with the *eyes*

than with the *ears*.   GERMAN PROVERB

People cannot help but reveal their true nature when Uriel is around. If they claim to be honest, they should not lie to anyone. If they claim to be faithful, they should never have cheated on anyone. If they tell you that they are wealthy, they should not have borrowed money from anyone. If they say that family is important to them, they should not neglect the one that they have. Listen to what they say but believe what they do; if you are suspicious, ask Uriel to confirm whether they have been truthful or not. He will place the answer immediately in your mind. You may not always like it, but it will always be correct. His light of truth shines into the most private areas of each and all our lives to reveal the secrets that people may try to hide. He will tell you if someone is lying to you.

Angela "I met a guy last year who seemed to be a good bet. He turned up in a flashy BMW and took me to really nice restaurants. He had his own business and he said he had been searching for two years for someone to share his life. I thought it was odd that he never invited me to go to his house but apart from that everything was wonderful, at first. However, it didn't take long for the fancy restaurants to disappear and soon I was feeding him and running around after him. To cut a long story short, the car belonged to a friend, he only borrowed it to impress me, the business was a franchise for which he was in debt, and he had been living with his girlfriend for two years. His feet soon came off my couch and didn't touch the floor on the way out of my door."

... another sad tale of someone who did not consult Uriel during the dating process.

On a first date nobody but you need know that you have the powerful Archangel Uriel batting on your team. Besides, if you meet someone for the first time and you tell them, "I've asked an angel to come along," you may get a strange reaction. Not everyone is as aware of angels as you are. Unless, of course, your date is also an angel fan, in which case they may have invited Uriel along to help them too.

As soon as possible after the date has ended, take stock of what happened. Don't waste time wondering what they thought of you; it's too late to do anything about that now. Instead take out your Raphael List and give your date marks out of ten for each characteristic. This is where Uriel's gift for clarity is useful, again, as he will guide you to be honest with yourself.

You may wish to score them higher than they deserve in some areas because you have fallen in love with their cute smile or their sexy butt; however, giving them extra points now will only cause trouble later. If you exaggerate their qualities, you are only lying to yourself. Rating a date in this way removes the emotion that often clouds judgment when you have just met someone. That cute smile or sexy butt can really get in the way and make you lose all your common sense, but if you have a list of traits that are important you can focus on these and not on superficial attributes. You may wish to add "cute smile" or "sexy butt" to your list but it is too late. You set out with a

Angel Advice
first date don'ts

1 Wear lime green —very few people can pull it off.

2 Interrupt—people like to talk and be listened to.

3 Moan, about anyone or anything.

4 Order nachos—they are impossible to eat and look cool.

5 Drink till you can't stand up.

6 Flirt with the waiters/waitresses.

7 Crack jokes—unless you are good at it.

Angel Advice

signs that they are not right for you

1 They can't remember your name.

2 You can't remember their name.

3 You felt like you were starring in a Woody Allen film.

4 You wanted to go home early.

5 They spent the whole of the date on their phone.

6 You deliberately lost their cell phone number.

7 They scored minus on most of your Raphael List.

particular intention and you cannot change it now. Using your Raphael List truthfully will make sure that you concentrate on the things that are important to you and not just whether they slurped their soup or not (unless, of course, you put "Expert soup-eater" high up on your list). People who have used their Raphael List report a sense of detachment and clarity that really changed the way that they dated. They were able to avoid the myth of chemistry and look for something more solid instead.

Another good way to judge the success of the date and your wish (or otherwise) for a second one is to analyze how you actually felt both during it and afterward. Again, Uriel can help you with this. Even if some things went wrong (you spilled the wine, you sneezed sauce all over them ... whatever) you still enjoyed the experience and would love to do it again. These are some of the questions to ask yourself after the date:

—Did I enjoy the date?
—Did they make me feel good?
—Was it easy to smile, laugh, talk, listen, and even relax with them?
—Did I enjoy being with them?
—Do I want to tell my friends about them?
—Did I feel enhanced by the experience, or lessened by it?
—Would I do it again?

Asking the questions is one thing, but actually accepting the answers is another. It is always tempting to fall into the trap of self-delusion, where you are happy to lie to yourself: "Yes, I felt great when they made fun of my nose"; "Of course I enjoyed listening to them talk about their ex"; "I would see them tomorrow if they weren't seeing someone else." Being honest with yourself is being kind to yourself and Uriel can help. He will clear away any self-delusion and replace it with honesty, no matter how painful this may be. At this point the pain will pass quickly; if you continue, it will only get worse. Unfortunately sometimes we excel at dismissing Uriel's answers and deluding ourselves into believing something that simply isn't true. How often have you heard people say, "I should have known he was no good," or "I had a feeling she was lying to me"? Ignoring Uriel is never a good idea. At best it means that success will take longer, at worst it leads to heartbreak and recriminations.

Ignoring Uriel's advice can be a costly experience, and yet we all do it. Somehow we think that we know better, so we push those nagging doubts to the back of our minds and only later, when things go wrong, do we realize that we should have listened to his guidance. How many broken hearts could have been prevented if only everyone paid more attention to Uriel? And yet the angels never judge us or withdraw their support. Making mistakes is part of the human condition, so when we stubbornly go off following our own opinions, the angels still come with us to take care of us and (usually) pick up the pieces afterward.

Fools rush in where *angels* fear to tread.

ALEXANDER POPE

A first date does not have to be daunting. You don't have to be terrified, try too hard, act like an idiot, or kick yourself all the way home. You can now take advantage of the immense power and wisdom of Archangel Uriel. With just one request he can make you relaxed, confident, assured, and fascinating. He will give you insight and the astuteness to make sure that you do not fall for any lies. There really is no better angel to have on your side than Uriel when going on a date, so make sure you take him with you. Afterward he will help you to assess how you feel and what you want to happen next. Then he can hand you over to Archangel Jophiel, who looks after the next part of the dating process.

Chapter Five

Wanting the One

Miracles do happen. Miracles happen because Archangel Jophiel makes them happen. This is good news if you are looking for love. There are times when it feels like nothing less than a miracle will do. If you've been on a thousand failed dates, if you've sat by the phone for hours, if you're about to despair, it is time for Jophiel to come to the rescue. Jophiel can manipulate people and situations to make sure you get your share of love action. As we said in Chapter Three, sitting back and doing nothing will get you nowhere, but if you work with Jophiel you will be able to turn your dreams of love into reality.

Archangel Jophiel

The Miracle Worker

Jophiel means "The Beauty of God" and she is in charge of creating beauty in the universe. She inspires creative thoughts and endeavors, including relationships, so she is the angel responsible for people falling in love. Her energy is a pale yellow like a primrose so you may be drawn to this color when she is having an influence in your world. She is also famous for working miracles, so nothing is impossible with Jophiel.

The *golden rule* is that there are *no* golden rule

GEORGE BERNARD SHAW

Jophiel does not have strict dating "rules." There are no rules except your rules – whatever is right for you *is* right. There is no universal law that says you cannot make the first move, or that you should refuse to answer the phone. If somebody telephones you, there is no need to wait a day before you call them back. If they ask you out, don't pretend that you are busy seeing friends, then sit alone at home feeling miserable. If your heart leaps into your throat when they call you, then answer the phone before you choke. If you want to speak to someone, don't endure the agony of not doing so, just pick up the phone and say, "Hi, I was just thinking of you and wanted to give you a quick call." That way everybody knows where they stand. Even if they don't answer the phone, at least you tried and you don't have to spend all day wondering. Sticking to dating "rules" might (or might not) make your dream date come running, but it can also make you really unhappy in the meantime. There are just too many different people in this world for one set of rules to work for everybody. "Playing by the rules" is really "playing games," so only do it if you are prepared to lose as well as win. Personally I believe that love is too important to be played around with, so I would rather be upfront and truthful. When you date with Jophiel you follow only one rule, and that is to be true to yourself.

So you have met someone, you have been on a first date, and you are wondering what happens next? You are in one of four possible scenarios:

    —Neither of you ever wants to set eyes on the other again.
    —You want to see them again, but they don't want to see you.
    —They want to see you again but you don't want to see them.
    —You both want to see each other again.

Only one of these will lead to a second date. If the first option is true, then there's no problem; you don't have to do anything. Don't explain, don't apologize, don't look for closure. Just put it down to experience and move on. If the second option is where you are, then life is more complicated. Despite the enormous changes in the role of women in society over the past fifty years, sadly the man still "does the running." As annoying as this is, if a woman does the running, the man usually runs in the opposite direction. It is all to do with man being a hunter, and (for all the progress that women have made) you can't change fifty thousand years of evolution in just fifty short ones. So if you are the girl, you just have to sit and wait for the phone to ring. If he doesn't call, he is not interested. Plain and simple. He isn't playing it cool or recharging his cell phone, and he hasn't lost your number or been kidnapped by bandits. He just doesn't want to see you again. Sorry. I know this sucks but there is absolutely nothing that you can do about it. You cannot make someone fall in love with you just because it is what you want. You are only in control of how you feel, not how they feel. If you spend every waking moment thinking about them but they are busy thinking about work/football/shopping/someone else, then you are suffering from unrequited love. You have my sympathy. Unrequited love is an incredibly painful feeling. It is a mild form of grief, because you long for something that you cannot have, and you mourn for a future that will never happen. You need help.

Angel Advice
post-date worries

Women/*Men*

1 He won't call. *She won't return my call.*

2 My mother won't like him. *She'll have a mother.*

3 He is too good for me. *She is not good enough for me.*

4 He'll break my heart. *She'll dump me.*

5 He'll never commit. *She'll get needy.*

6 He only wants to sleep with me. *She might not sleep with me.*

7 Will it last forever? *Which soccer team does she support?*

Stages of *infatuation*

1 The lightning bolt that throws you off balance. A look, a gesture, a smile, a comment, or an incredible body part—who knows when or how it happens, but you are struck by Cupid's arrow right between the eyes. Bull's-eye.

2 Next comes the obsessive thinking. Some people confess to spending up to 90 percent of their time just thinking about the object of their desire, which doesn't leave much room for thinking about anything else.

3 Then there is the longing. The aching to see them again, which makes you grumpy, short-tempered, and even physically nauseous.

4 This is followed by the scheming, as you rearrange everything in your life in order to be with them. You manipulate and maneuver situations just so that you can breathe the same air as them.

Nothing takes the taste out o
unrequited love.

5 Each precious moment that you spend in their presence takes on extra significance. You are convinced that they are funnier, smarter, and more gorgeous than anyone else that you have ever met.

6 You now begin to believe that they are soooo desirable that it is only a matter of time before someone else gets their claws into them and steals them from you. You start to panic.

7 Delight and doubt now fill your life in equal measure. One moment there is hope and the next uncertainty. That is the exhausting and exquisite form of torture known as infatuation.

peanut butter quite like

CHARLIE BROWN

John "About a year ago I fell in love. I have absolutely no chance, because I am gay and he isn't. On Valentine's Day I sent him an e-mail card and to my horror he worked out that it was from me. I fully expected him to tell everyone what an idiot I had been, but instead he was very supportive. He said he was sorry that I had these feelings for him when it was impossible for him to feel the same way about me. Instead of helping my problem this only made it worse as I saw him as a decent human being as well as a gorgeous hunk. He is everything that I could ever want in a boyfriend and I will never find anyone to measure up to him."

Only someone who has been through the anguish of infatuation and unrequited love knows how awful it can be, so I know what I am talking about. When I was seventeen I had a huge crush on someone who shall remain nameless. I followed him home from school, walked past his house to see if he was in, melted when he looked my way, prayed that he would dance with me at the disco, and was convinced that he was my future husband. Guess why he has to remain nameless—because I genuinely can't remember his name.

Time is a great healer, but Jophiel is an even better one. Always remember that she is a great miracle worker. As unbelievable as it may seem, if you ask for Jophiel's help, she will calm your troubled emotions and help you to survive unrequited love. She really can work miracles, so she will ease your longing and take away the burden by making your heart lighter. Other things in your life will begin to seem important to you again and I promise that one morning you will wake up and the object of your infatuation will not be the first thing on your

There are few people who are not *ashamed* of their love affairs when the *infatuation* is over.

FRANÇOIS DE LA ROCHEFOUCAULD

mind. When you are feeling more normal you may be able to see why you fell so far so fast. You will probably realize that they are not the walking god/goddess that you thought they were and you will probably feel a little foolish. There is nothing wrong with that. Getting something wrong can be very useful; understanding your mistakes can prevent them from happening again.

Although infatuation is regarded by many as a stupid waste of time, it is really one of Jophiel's miracles and an important part of the dating experience. It means that you feel deeply about someone else and put their interests and welfare before your own, and that is the beginning of unconditional love. Even with its undeniable lows, infatuation brings with it extreme highs of excitement and pleasure. You really know that you are alive when you are infatuated. Infatuation is defined in the dictionary as "inspired with an extravagant passion"; everyone should know how that feels at least once in their lifetime.

Jophiel has a certain "Wow!" factor about her. If you have ever had an experience that has made you go "Wow! How did that happen?" or "Wow! That's amazing," you have been zapped by Jophiel. Often it is Jophiel who is responsible for that incredible "love at first sight" phenomenon.

1 Whenever you see them you lose all feeling in your legs.

2 George Clooney/Angelina Jolie is suddenly just "okay."

3 Sad songs on the radio seem to be written about you (and them).

4 You stand still in the grocery store just thinking about them.

5 You have homicidal thoughts if they are affectionate to anyone else.

6 You spend hours getting that "casual" look just right.

7 You build a life-size model of them out of papier-mâché for your bedroom—okay, this is taking it too far and may lead to your arrest.

Gary "When I first laid eyes on my future wife I thought, 'Oh s**t.'
I knew immediately that this was the woman I wanted to spend the rest
of my life with and it scared the hell out of me. Don't ask me how I knew.
It was a done deal from that moment on."

If you are the object of someone else's infatuation, then you are stuck in
scenario number three. This is probably the trickiest situation to be in, because
even though it is fabulous for the ego, it is also fraught with problems. If you
see them again you are stringing them along with false hope; if you avoid them
you are prolonging the agony; if you dump them you are breaking their heart.
You cannot win. Probably the worst thing that you can do is carry on dating
them knowing that you are not really keen. Many people do this while they
wait for something better to come along. You may know somebody who has
a boyfriend/girlfriend but who always keeps their options open. I call these
people "sailor daters" as they like to keep a dinghy while they wait for their
boat to come in.

Again, we come back to honesty. If you continue a relationship knowing that
they are more involved than you are, that you do not want to invest as much
emotionally as they have, then you are putting off the day when the truth will
have to be told. Procrastination is cowardly. Do not avoid seeing them, evade
their phone calls, or invent reasons why you are too busy to meet up. Be honest
and end it quickly even if (horror of horrors) it means that you will be single
for a while afterward. The fear of being alone should not keep you in a bad
relationship. Being with "someone" is not good enough if you are serious about
finding "the one," so don't sell yourself short.

Letting someone down is never easy but, yet again, it is so much easier if you
tell the truth. This doesn't mean listing all the reasons that you find someone
physically abhorrent, but it does mean being upfront about your feelings and
your intentions for the future. To some extent this is the classic "It's not you, it's
me" scenario. It's not the fact that they smell of cabbages that is the problem—

is the fact that you don't like the smell of cabbages. You know that one day they will meet someone who adores everything about cabbages who will make them very happy.

Under these circumstances, I'm sure you would be grateful for a massive dose of angel help—this is where Jophiel's miracles come in again. She can take the sting out of the awkward situation and even prepare the other person for the bad news. I have known people to dread the "I don't know how to tell you this" conversation, only to find that Jophiel had got there first. The "dumped" was amazingly philosophical and the "dumper" almost annoyed that there weren't more tears.

A quick word of warning here: Before you decide that you don't want to see someone again, just take a moment to ask our old friend Uriel if you are doing the right thing. As the angel of enlightenment he will clarify whether you are dumping this person for the right reasons or not. Remember the girl who was afraid of disappointing her mother? She turned down a second date with several men just because she thought Mommy wouldn't approve. Then again you might be scared of being hurt, so you decide to get in first and do the dumping before you get dumped. There is a false satisfaction in being able to say, "I ended it," if you don't know what you've ended. For all you know they thought you were the best thing since chocolate ice cream and they had every intention of staying around for a long time. Uriel will stop you from doing something that you may regret and may even give you the greatest gift of all: a chance of happiness.

Most people are not completely honest on a first date. They do not reveal everything about themselves. Why should they? (You haven't confessed about stealing that towel from the hotel yet.) Intimacy takes time and as a "rule of thumb" it takes three meetings before a person opens up enough for you to make an informed judgment about their true character. That is why Jophiel has a "Three Date Policy." If you like someone and you feel that you want to see them again, give it three dates (at least) before you make any important decisions. People can completely change their opinion of someone (for better or for worse) from the end of date one to the end of date three, so give it a little time.

So we come to the fourth possible scenario on the list: You both wish to see each other again. Okay, so you are infatuated, but then (fortunately) so is the other person. You are both grinning like sentimental fools. It is green for go. Cue the fireworks and the orchestra.

Chapter Six

Getting the One

Mutual infatuation is a blissful, crazy existence. It is the closest thing to delicious insanity. It is also very dangerous. Standing on the edge of a new romance is like teetering on a cliff edge without a parachute. It is exciting and frightening at the same time. You need Ariel to give you a push.

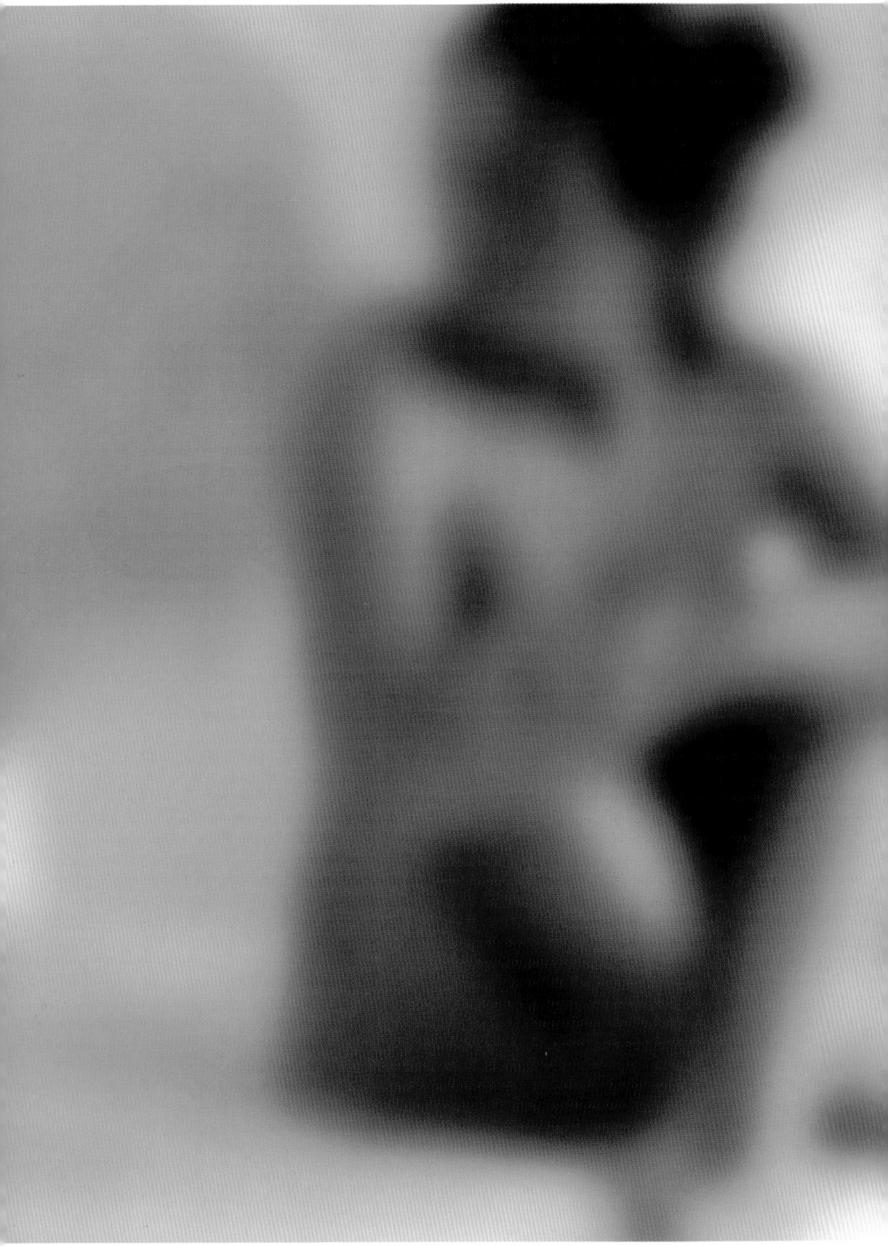

Archangel Ariel

The Magician

Ariel is known as the "Lioness of God" and she represents many of the qualities of this animal: elegance, daring, sleekness, nobility, and bravery. And you need to be brave if you are going to take a leap into the unknown. Ariel's energy is a pale pink color, so if you surround yourself with this you will help to bring her energy through. You may also begin to see images of lions and lionesses or be drawn to animal prints when Ariel's influence is with you.

Taking a leap into the unknown of a new relationship requires courage, but Ariel can help you with this. All you have to do is ask her and she will sprinkle her magic dust all around you. Ariel is known as the "angel magician" because she works with divine magic to bring about your wildest dreams. She can turn your life into a fairytale place where everything seems slightly unreal. You may find yourself saying and doing the most unexpected and spontaneous things: walking in the rain at midnight, sitting under a cold starry sky, splashing in puddles, staying in bed all day, and all the other silly things that people do when they are in love.

Ariel will free you from the restraints of the ego so that you can release your inner child. This is why new lovers act like children; they are caught up in a powerful yet mysterious attraction that can override all common sense and turn the ordinary into the surreal. Fortunately, you are both infected with the same malaise, so this is a different story altogether from unrequited love. Life is grand when you are both equally insane. Unfortunately, most of what you do right now will annoy other people intensely (not that you will care one bit). You will probably insist on holding hands, call each other pet names, talk in baby voices, and laugh at anything either of you says. You have joined the couples that irritated you so much when you were single in Chapter One. People who are mutually infatuated always get on everyone else's nerves.

Mike "I really wanted to see my girlfriend one night, but my car was in the workshop and not likely to be ready for a week. I decided that was not going to stop me, so I got on my mom's old bike and cycled the five miles to my girlfriend's house. She opened the door with a huge grin on her face that made my heart jump into my mouth. I told her that I had ridden the whole way just to see her eyes, and she told me that I was a total idiot."

Love is being *stupid* together.   PAUL VALERY

At this time in your life you are closest to feeling like an angel. You can love unconditionally, continually, and selflessly. Love is all-consuming, it is glorious, and it is ephemeral. Ariel will help you to focus on your feelings right now and to enjoy every single moment.

Quite often people spoil the "now" worrying about the future. "What if she dumps me?" "When will he tell me that he loves me?" "Where is this going?" Even in our most magnificent, life-affirming moments we allow doubt and self-sabotage to creep in and spoil everything. You will always feel insecure when you are in love because someone else has the power to hurt you. The very act of loving makes you unsure: unsure of the other person, unsure of the future, even unsure of yourself most of the time. You can't sleep; you don't want to eat; you can't concentrate; you neglect work, household chores, and your friends. Everything seems different; nothing is normal anymore. Congratulations, you are falling in love, and for a period of time you will be totally crazy. In fact there is not much point in reading the rest of this chapter because you won't take anything in until this phase begins to recede in about seven months' time.

Sometimes falling in love with someone can be so scary. You don't feel in control of your emotions and you may begin to think that you are going around the bend. If you don't like this then you can ask Ariel to slow the process down. She will then put the breaks on your emotional roller coaster until you feel back in control. Of course, if you are relishing the craziness then just sit back and enjoy the ride.

The period of mutual infatuation can last seven days, seven weeks, or seven months, depending on the two people involved.

Seven Days. This is the firework rocket of infatuation. It is a brief, intense, dazzling, spectacular display of emotion that ends with a bang and fizzles out. You may get superficial burns, but usually there is no lasting damage or scar. This kind of infatuation is a blast of emotional intensity that is like a romantic slap around the chops saying, "Hey, wake up and feel something."

Seven Weeks. This is the cruise missile of infatuation. There is no escaping it, as it finds its target with deadly accuracy. It is lethal, powerful, effective, and usually expensive, both financially and emotionally. If it impacts, it causes widespread damage and bad wounds. This period of infatuation should be taken very seriously, as it can have a knock-on effect on every other area of your life: your career, your friendships, and your future. It is a romantic headlock that says, "You're in this and you have to feel something."

Seven Months. This is the space rocket of infatuation. It blasts off with a tremendous irresistible force, it is fueled by intense burning and it is impressive, cosmic, scary, and out of this world. If it implodes, the fallout is horrendous and the scars take a long time to heal. This infatuation will either take you to the stars or make you splash down to earth without a parachute. This is a romantic knockout that says, "You have never felt like this before."

Communication can be a big problem when you are first falling in love with someone. Insecurity stops you from saying things, revealing your feelings, and even believing that it is happening. "It's too good to be true." "It will all go wrong." "I'll get my heart broken." You may be trying to protect your delicate emotions, but self-sabotaging thoughts all come from fear; they are not necessarily real. Often a good relationship fails because of poor communication. Only the angels are telepathic, so there will come a point when one of you has to be brave enough to say what has to be said. Ask Archangel Michael for the

ourage, and Archangel Gabriel for the words,
o tell the person that you love exactly how you
eel. Okay, so your heart may get broken; but
hen again, it may not. This is the time to take
a giant leap of faith and trust in your angels.
Believe that they have sent you this magnificent
gift of happiness and be thankful.

You are allowed to enjoy this period of crazy lust
and loving to the full and Ariel is just the angel who
can help you do this. She is the "Angel of Nature," a
beautiful being of light who helps us to understand
the natural rhythms of the earth, trees, flowers,
ocks, and soil. If you ask Ariel, she will help you to
connect with nature and be your natural self. One
specific area where she can assist is with sex.
Despite popular opinion, being angelic is not about
being chaste. Angels are playful and they know
hat we humans have physical bodies that bring
us pleasure. Angels are never judgmental, so they
neither approve nor disapprove of our sexual
activities. No angel is going to wag a proverbial
finger at you for having sex if it brings you great
oy, satisfaction, and fulfillment. In particular, Ariel
s an earthy, sensual presence who can remove any
inhibitions or prudishness you might have, so that
you really enjoy having sex.

Healthy, *lusty* sex is
wonderful.   JOHN WAYNE

The prerequisite for *making love* is to like someone *enormously.* HELEN GURLEY BROWN

Sex is fun. Sex is fabulous. Sex is fantastic. Animals don't have our hang-ups about sex. You never see a dog blushing and running to hide behind a bush. Humans are the only creatures who get embarrassed about sex, and isn't it strange that something so natural, so beautiful, and so widespread should be so taboo? After all, none of us would be here to get embarrassed if our parents had not had sex. Having sex is a normal activity, but it is best when experienced in a safe, trusting situation with integrity on both sides. It is also an important aspect of any relationship and should be treated with respect. It is too easy to dismiss sex as just a release of physical desires, when it is much more than that. The sexual act is a very intimate joining of two bodies, signifying far more than just a mutual attraction. What you are really saying when you have sex with someone is, "I like you enough to let you get as close to me as is physically possible"—that should mean something to you and to them. If you value yourself, you will be choosy about who gets this close. And it goes without saying that the person who does get to share your time, your space, and your body is very lucky.

Now we get to that old chestnut—when should you first have sex with someone? Again, there are no "set rules." If you want to rip each other's clothes off the first time that you meet, that's fine. If you prefer to wait, that's fine too. Everybody is different and only you are responsible for your own decisions and your own body. However, if you adopt Jophiel's Three Date Policy from Chapter Five, you will want to wait until you have had at least three meetings with someone before you get naked with them. Remember, people usually only reveal their true nature after three dates, so if you are happy to know their body before their mind, go for it. If not, wait. Ariel can give you the strength and courage to say "No," until you are happy to say "Yes." If the other person does not respect this, then they do not respect you. Waiting until you are ready sends out the message that you respect yourself and your body, you also respect them and their body, and you are serious about the future of the relationship. Plus, the anticipation is delicious and can sometimes be more enjoyable than the act itself.

You may need a little help moving from the lustful looking to the touchy-feely stage. There comes "the moment," like in the movies, when you are close enough to kiss ... what do you do? Kissing is not as easy as it looks on screen: there are noses, tongues, and breathing to consider. Too dry and you get stuck, too sloppy and you drool. How do you swallow anyway?

You may have guessed that there are **Kissing Angels** *who govern the activity of locking lips. As "the moment" approaches, just whisper a silent cry for help to the* **Kissing Angels** *and let them do the rest. They will maneuver you into the right positions and guide you so that you follow your "instincts" (angel messages) and enjoy a sexy kissing session.*

The best way to be sexy with a new lover is to be wildly confident. Before you panic, you will be glad to know that this can be made easier with angelic help. Fortunately, Ariel has the power to make you feel good about yourself and your body. One common fallacy is that other people have fabulous bodies that they love showing off. Some people may have fewer inhibitions than others, but nobody is totally happy with their body—nobody. Not even people who make a living from being gorgeous look in the mirror and love what they see. Men tend to be more self-forgiving than women in this respect, but it is still rare for a guy to strip off for the first time and feel 100 percent sure of himself. So take heart, if you are concerned about those extra pounds or that spot on your butt, your lover is too busy worrying about their own flaws to notice yours. Ariel can help with your self-consciousness about your body by refocusing you on the positive.

Angel Advice

bad reasons to have sex

1 You feel sorry for them.

2 The central heating is broken.

3 You want to brag about it later.

4 To prove that you love them.

5 There's nothing on television.

6 They begged, bullied, or blackmailed you.

7 All your friends are doing it and you feel left out.

Okay, so you may think that your nose is huge, but instead of making self-deprecating comments about it, simply don't mention it at all. Instead, draw attention to your long legs, your taut stomach, or whichever other part of your body you are reasonably happy with. Ask yourself, are you only attracted to people with perfect bodies? Have you ever fallen for someone who scored less than ten out of ten? I bet you have. It is not just physical flawlessness that counts, it is the whole package—the way they smile, the way they talk, the way they carry themselves—that matters more. None of us are angels, we all have good and bad parts, so accept your imperfections and move on.

There is another practical way that Ariel helps the "first time" to be a success and that is by guiding you to the best place and time for it to happen. If you have ever come close to ripping someone's clothes off but something (or someone) interrupted and it never happened, you can be sure that Ariel intervened. If you ask, she will orchestrate things so that the first time is more fur rugs and open fires than Ford transits and steamy windows. If you are too busy worrying about other stuff—the size of your nose, cellulite, waking the neighbors, or the gear stick—you will not be able to concentrate on the important bit, which is enjoying yourself. Ask Ariel to keep your self-confidence high and her magic powers will help you to lose your inhibitions and allow you to enjoy the most glorious, guilt-free sex.

Beauty is in the *heart* of the beholder.

AL BERNSTEIN

However, even Ariel cannot guarantee great sex the first time that you make love to someone—especially if you have lusted after them for a while. If you have fantasized about their gorgeous body, what a great lover they will be, and how many window-rattling orgasms you will have, you will be left feeling dissatisfied. It is going to be difficult for real life to measure up to your feverish imagination. You will probably both be too nervous, too self-conscious, too embarrassed, too many limbs everywhere, for it to resemble a scene out of your favorite sexy film. Sex is like anything else: The more you do it, the better you get at it. Highly erotic and deeply gratifying lovemaking takes practice, but boy, is it fun getting it right.

Terry "I was trying to be romantic, so I sprinkled rose petals all over the place and lit candles throughout the house. When we started to make love we were both so engrossed that neither of us spotted that the candles on the bedside table were too close. The bed was shaking (if you get what I mean) and so was the bedside table. You can guess what happened next. The candle fell over and landed on my leg. Hot wax burned my skin and the shock was too much. I yelled in agony. She thought I was in the throes of ecstasy and she joined in screaming and wailing. It was the most embarrassing moment of my life when I had to explain that it wasn't her but the candle that was making me hot. Still, I guess it's another example of not practicing safe sex."

I don't want to spoil the party but nothing stays the same; situations and emotions always change and this madness will not last. Despite six months being an unspoken code between lovers that things are now in the "serious" phase, if you believe this then you are suffering from a false sense of security.

Seven months is the usual time span of mutual infatuation in what is (euphemistically) termed a "serious" relationship.

Do not make the mistake of thinking that you are home and dry after six months. Just as you finally feel it is safe enough to wear your less sexy underwear, wham! Your lover drops the bombshell that it's all over. This is known as "The Seven Month Dump" and it is as cruel as it is commonplace. Then again you may be on the other side and find that after six months you are ready to make a bolt for the door. This is because Ariel's magic love dust is wearing off and you are sobering up to a romantic reality—you've had enough.

Infatuation is the electrifying spark that sets emotions aflame, but despite the sizzling frustration and fiery passion, it is just as likely to fizzle out as to warm your heart forever. When Ariel's magic love dust blows away, you will discover whether your mutual infatuation was a flash in the pan or a slow-burning furnace.

Chapter Seven

Loving the One

This book is all about how angels can help you to find the love of your life. You are now halfway through the book, so how is it going? By now you will know who you are and what you want. You know how to look for someone and how to be confident on a date; how to flirt, kiss, and be yourself. You know if someone is lying to you and you can assess how you feel about them. You can deal with unreturned feelings and unwanted attention. You can be sexy and have great sex. You are a dating demon.

The Lover

Chamuel's loving energy is a deep sensual pink
so you may feel an affinity with this color when
he is influencing your life. You can call on
Chamuel to help you to recognize real love, love
others, and boost your self-love so that you
know that you deserve only situations associated
with genuine feelings.

Before I met my husband I'd never *fallen* in love, though I'd *stepped* in it a few times.

RITA RUDNER

Surely you have got it all sorted out by now and you are happily settling into a great relationship with a wonderful person? What do you mean, "No, I'm not?" Clearly you are doing something wrong...

Well, not necessarily. Getting it right means nothing if you don't know what getting it wrong feels like. You have to go through some bad relationships in order to recognize a good one when it comes along. How will you know if this is the best person for you to spend the rest of your life with if you have nothing to compare them with? Dating is a bit like road-testing several automobiles until you find that dream car that we talked about in Chapter Three.

In today's world we are given more choice than ever before. Once there was only a loaf of bread at the neighborhood store, whereas now supermarket shelves groan with wholewheat, mixed grain, rye, pita, pumpernickel, ciabatta, focaccia, brioche, bagels, and sourdough bread. It's much the same with dating. Instead of pairing up with someone suitable from the same village, we can choose from the global village. This may make finding someone easier, but it also makes it harder to commit to just one person. How do you know while you are eating a wholemeal sandwich today that you won't feel like stuffed pita tomorrow? To get over the uncertainty of new love call on Archangel Chamuel.

Chamuel allows you to keep and hold loving thoughts, especially about others. He then provides you with ways to manifest these thoughts, to create harmony and love in your life. He will replace doubt and ambiguity with assurance. You will no longer feel the need to keep your options open just in case you get a chance to eat a Mongolian malt loaf. (No, it doesn't exist, but then neither does that super-enhanced lover that you are holding out for.) Wonderful relationships of all kinds happen when Chamuel gets involved. All you need to do is ask him to guide you and show you how to release any doubts or fears.

Andy "I've had long relationships before and am currently in a really good one. She's not my first love, but I don't think I've ever loved anyone more. We live together and that's fine, have good sex and all that, and there's nothing actually bad about the relationship. However, I sometimes feel as though I'm getting a bit bored and miss the guys' nights out. Just the thought of being single again seems good, from a freedom point of view. But if I were single again I'd more than likely regret it and at some point wish that I hadn't ended it at all. Is this the start of a breakup or just a classic case of wanting what you haven't got?"

The number of people who have trouble with commitment is going up and the finger is not just pointing at the male of the species. The single biggest reason for this is the acceptance of sex without commitment. It was not very long ago that if you wanted to have sex with someone, you had to marry them first. This may make teenagers giggle, but it's true. With greater sexual freedom came greater choice, hence less commitment.

Angel Advice
signs that you are afraid of commitment

1 You don't own an answering machine.

2 You date people who are already attached to someone else.

3 You send sympathy cards instead of wedding cards.

4 You write phone numbers in pencil.

5 You have never owned a pet.

6 You rent instead of buying.

7 You have half a dozen engagement rings in your drawer.

If you are not exactly sure what commitment means, in romantic terms it is an intention to share thoughts, feelings, time, experiences, and emotions with one other person exclusively and in perpetuity. There is no time limit or expiry date to commitment. It is not a case of "I promise to commit to you utterly until next Tuesday." Yes, situations and people change, and sometimes this change will bring about the end of a relationship, but at the beginning the intention for a commitment to last forever is pure. If you have problems with commitment, ask Chamuel to pour undiluted love into your heart so that you can commit yourself body and spirit to the relationship.

Susie "I would say that I am a commitment phobe and the idea of marriage or babies terrifies me. I could cope with living with someone and I did for a while but he started to say that he wanted us to get married. He was worried that he would be an old dad and I insist that I will not have children till I am at least thirty. But I am worried that when I do get to thirty I will move the goalposts to thirty-five. I ended it with him, which I know wasn't really fair. All I can say is that I am afraid of being unhappy and feeling trapped or dependent on someone. My parents separated years ago but have not got divorced and it is partly having seen what happened to them that makes me afraid of marrying anyone."

If you are already sold on your romance but your partner is dragging their heels, again Chamuel can help. He will suggest ways to you that you can lovingly move the relationship forward. One very simple way is to set a test. Suggest that you both go on a trip together at some time in the future. This clearly shows your intention still to be part of the relationship at that time, and their reaction will tell you if they intend the same. What we are looking for here is a ready agreement and a degree of enthusiasm for the trip. If they dodge making firm arrangements and leave you guessing as to whether they will or won't make the trip, then you are looking at a person who has a problem with commitment. They could be a "hunter" or one of the "hunted."

The Hunter. Some people enjoy the thrill of the chase so much that they get addicted; they become infatuation junkies. When Ariel's magic love dust wears off they look for another hit. Settling down into the next phase of romance just doesn't compare with the adrenaline rush of meeting someone new.

The Hunted. Other people are afraid of being trapped. Scared of being "stuck" with one person for the rest of their lives, they run like frightened rabbits for the nearest bolthole. These people are commitment phobes. For them, settling down is the equivalent of being tied down, so they keep on moving or hide.

Hunters and the hunted use similar methods when dating:

–They are overenthusiastic at first and pursue you relentlessly.
–They won't take "No" for an answer and profess undying love.
–When they catch you, they suddenly become much less interested.
–They never talk about the future.
–They say that they need "space."
–They disrespect you until you end it (saving them the trouble).
–They disappear only to come back and start the process all over again.

Sound familiar? Commitment-shy partners are often late or cancel at the last minute; they go missing; they don't return phone calls; they feign a terrible memory. It is tempting to dismiss this as charming (especially at first), but if it continues beyond the seven months of infatuation you have to ask yourself what is really going on. Chamuel's name means "He who sees God" and his pure vision can be used to help us see others more clearly. This may mean opening your eyes to things that you have been blind to in the first phase of the relationship. At this stage in the romance you will see three possible options:

–Your partner will commit to the relationship in the future by themselves.
–Your partner will commit to the relationship in the future for a reason.
–Your partner will never commit to the relationship.

Stages of Commitment

1 Looking lustfully.

2 Giving gifts.

3 Holding hands.

4 Sharing sheets.

5 Meeting friends.

6 Doing do-it-yourself.

7 Twin tattoos.

Stages of Noncommitment

1 Ongoing options.

2 Springing surprises.

3 Avoiding answers.

4 Clearing conscience.

5 Forgetting faithfulness.

6 Deceiving deliberately.

7 Escaping easily.

The difference between *involvement* and *commitment* is like ham and eggs. The chicken is *involved*; the pig is *committed*.

MARTINA NAVRATILOVA

It is fair to say that everyone reaches the final stage of commitment in their own time, so sometimes you need to be patient. Chamuel can give you the tolerance you need to make allowances for someone else and accept them for who they are. He can pour his grace into you so that you feel calmer and more at peace. It is amazing how he can remove the frustration and tension from a situation, just by influencing how you feel. With Chamuel's limitless ability to create love, he will supply you with the patience to let someone just be themselves. Once you have made this shift inside, it will show on the outside in the way that you act toward your partner. Ironically, this may be the very thing that makes them commit to you. In other words, stop pushing the river and float along instead, trusting that Chamuel will keep you safe.

There may be a catalyst that gives your partner the final push and makes them commit; maybe some friends get married, a new job comes along that means relocation, or perhaps a baby is on the way. If something happens that makes them feel that they are ready to make the same pledge as you, then great. If not, don't be tempted to employ any strategies to get your partner to commit—they simply won't work. There is no point in threatening desertion, financial ruin, blackmail, or bodily harm. Think about it, if you have to coerce someone to commit to you, why are you with them anyway? Twisting their arm in the short term does not mean that they will stick it out for a lifetime.

Angel Advice
good reasons to be in a relationship

1 Sex on tap.

2 You get invited to more dinner parties.

3 You don't need to wear your best underwear all the time.

4 Makes you, your partner, and (usually) your parents happy.

5 Halves the bills.

6 Disturbs exes.

7 No need to date anymore.

A relationship is like a *shark,* it has to move forward constantly or it *dies.*   WOODY ALLEN

The one thing that will convince your partner is to show them that you love them. If you give love you get it back. This may seem ridiculously obvious but if you are frustrated with someone you project anger onto that person; consequently, you appear as a nasty, bitter piece of work (and let's face it, who would want to be around someone like that?). Your partner needs to know that you are a loving person whom they can love back. Chamuel will help you experience the deepest feelings of love and then express those feelings to your partner. This does not mean that you will have a complete personality change and suddenly start laughing at all their jokes, buying them expensive presents, and baking cookies with their name on them. If you become a doormat, they will simply wipe their feet on you—on the way out. Instead, be true to yourself (and to them) by loving yourself (and them) with integrity.

As time goes by, if nothing changes, if you have invested a lot of time, emotion, belief, and energy in someone and it is not being returned, if you really are fed up with the situation, you could consider the last resort—the ultimatum. Always think long and hard before you use an ultimatum because (as the word suggests) it really is the final option. Calling upon Chamuel's infinite love will enable you to handle the whole event with grace and compassion. He will help you to prepare what you are going to say and how you will say it, which will not only make the experience easier for you but will also let your partner know that you are serious. Chamuel will insure that:

—You are not aggressive or threatening.
—You are responsible for your feelings and why you feel them.
—You explain why you are dissatisfied and unhappy.

—You list the things that you want to change.
—You suggest solutions as to how these
   changes will happen.
—You give a time frame in which this must be
   achieved.
—You are very clear about the consequence of
   change not happening.

Only ever use an ultimatum when you have reached
a stage where you are willing to accept either
outcome. Yes, you could get the result that you
want, but it is fifty/fifty that you won't; if this
unhappy event occurs, then you must follow the
ultimatum through. There is no point in telling
someone to step up to the plate and ignoring it
when they don't. Empty ultimatums are like cheap
Easter eggs—they are hollow and unsatisfying. If
you tell someone to change or you will leave, then
if they don't change you must leave. It is as simple
as that. Staying merely tells them that you are
prepared to accept the situation and subjugate your
happiness to theirs. If you are stuck in a one-sided
relationship ask Chamuel to give you the courage to
make the break. Because he is so kind he will
surround you with loving energy, which will give
you the strength to put your own heart and
happiness first.

So many people stay in a relationship hoping
that "things will get better." They very rarely do.
Some relationships stay in this state of hopeful
inadequacy for years, with no change.

Angel Advice
signs that you are
in love

1 You carry a
picture of them in
your purse/wallet.

2 You ache to see
them.

3 Their name is the
best name ... ever.

4 You go to the
grocery store
together.

5 You file away
jokes/stories to tell
them.

6 You don't have to
pretend.

7 There is no future
without them in it.

One person says, "I need this to make me happy," and the other person says, "I don't, so tough." The first person stays unhappy and dissatisfied, while the other carries on regardless. If it becomes clear that the person you are dating has no intention of changing or of committing exclusively to you now or in the future, simply get your coat and leave. Ending the relationship may make your partner realize that they do want to commit to you, but don't hold your breath. If they come running after you claiming that they made a mistake, that you are the best thing that ever happened to them, and that they are now ready to commit, make sure they mean it. Get proof. Never end a relationship expecting (or hoping) that this will happen. Be prepared to walk away with your head held high, not looking back over your shoulder. If you are single again, give yourself a little time to dry off before jumping back into the dating pool again. Reconnect with your friends and rediscover all the joys of singledom that we celebrated in Chapter One.

However, if you find yourself with someone who is ready to settle down, you can both take things to the next level. Whether it happened gradually or came as a bolt from the blue, you both want to be with each other, you cannot face being parted, and you are both ready to commit to the relationship. Congratulations. You are not just falling in love, you are well and truly wallowing in it.

To *love* is to receive a glimpse of *heaven.*

KAREN SUNDE

Chapter Eight

Keeping the One

If Chamuel helps people to fall in love, then Daniel is the angel who keeps them in love. If Chamuel makes you warm and fuzzy, then Daniel makes you cool, calm, and collected. He is concerned with the dynamics of each and every personal relationship, how people relate to each other, and how this changes over time. If you think of your romance as business, then you can imagine Daniel as a consultant who reviews, advises, and makes changes so that your particular "Love Inc" is a success.

Archangel Daniel

The Partner

Daniel is known as the angel who looks after marriage. Call upon him if you are planning a wedding to make sure that all the arrangements go smoothly. He will also help the marriage to be fulfilling and successful. He fosters feelings of respect, admiration, and loyalty. His name means "God is my Judge" and his energy vibrates with lime green, so look out for this color when he is working with and for you.

Angel Advice

**things that women
don't understand
about men**

1 Why plasma
screens and baseball
are important.

2 Why they fight.

3 Why they can't see
dirt.

4 Why they always
want a different car.

5 Why they collect
toolboxes and
gadgets.

6 Why the thought of
two girls is so great.

7 Why they won't
talk about "us."

The first piece of expert advice from Daniel is never to expect a member of the opposite sex to be like you. There was a brief period of time around the mid-seventies when it was fashionable to believe that everybody was the same, regardless of gender. Everyone grew their hair long, wore flares, and overdid the blue eye shadow. Of course, this was a complete waste of time as the two sexes will never be alike.

If you are in a heterosexual relationship, do yourself a favor and accept that you and your "other half" are very different. Some people hope that their partner will change and become more like them, and although it is true that couples who have been together for many years do grow more like each other, it is more important to accept that men and women are not the same and never will be. Hoping that one will morph into the other is like asking a cat to bark. Women do not come from Venus and men are not Martians, but we are two very different types of earthlings.

I *love* the idea of there being
two sexes, don't you?

JAMES THURBER

Keith "The only thing Kelly and I fight about is money. She is hopeless at budgeting. Of course I knew this when I met her, but when we were saving up to put a deposit down on the house she went out and bought a very expensive purse. I was furious. I was scrimping and saving, not buying myself anything, and not going out, and she went and blew a week's salary. She didn't even need the purse. We had a fight about it and of course she cried, so I felt bad. She offered to take the purse back, but I didn't want to seem to be tight so she kept it. I must admit she did get better after that and she cut down on the shopping, but she is still no good with money. If she's got it, she spends it, so I have to watch her."

Embracing the fact that your lover is different from you is giving them the gift of acceptance—and giving yourself a break. However, the fundamental differences between men and women cause havoc with romantic relationships, which is exactly what they are meant to do. If men and women were the same, there would never be any cause for conflict. As much as you may dislike arguments and fights, they help you learn about your relationship and each other. If you can deal with your differences, your romance will survive and flourish. This is where Daniel comes in. Like any consultant he can provide a clear overview of how your relationship works, so that you can manage it better. Just like in business, this is a diagram of your love affair.

The love affair chart

Love Zone. During the first seven months of a romance, when you are infatuated with each other, you usually wallow in the "Love Zone." This is where we all want to be most of the time. It is the pink, fluffy state of loving and being loved. This is Ariel's and Chamuel's territory of love, laughter, sex, fun, cuddles, and a mutual fan club.

Battle Zone. Inevitably there will be times when one of you transgresses—she flirts with another man, he goes out with the guys, she gets drunk, he forgets an anniversary, etc. Whatever the cause, the effect is the same: One person feels badly treated and consequently moves into the Battle Zone. This is Daniel's territory of conflict resolution. Here, the victim employs various tactics: nagging, blaming, accusing, or letting rip with both barrels. The other person is dragged into the Battle Zone whether they like it or not. Many people are afraid of this because they think their relationship is vulnerable there, but if you are both actively striving for a solution then you are "working" at the partnership. If you ask for it, Daniel's influence can help you to communicate calmly and compassionately, reach an understanding, and move back into the Love Zone together. The sooner you do this the better, as the more time spent in the Battle Zone, the more likely it is that one of you will move into the Retreat Zone.

Retreat Zone. This is the real danger area for a relationship. Once you move into this zone you have given up trying to solve the problem and are emotionally halfway out the door. Ironically, the tension and anger seem to die down at this stage, but, far from getting better, the relationship is slowly falling apart. One of you may stay in the Battle Zone valiantly trying to sort things out, or maybe even move back into the Love Zone mistakenly thinking that everything is better. Meanwhile the other person stays in the Retreat Zone and plans their escape.

Most people in a healthy relationship spend the first two years moving between the Love and Battle Zones. This is a normal process through which both of you challenge, debate, compromise, and accept things for the good of the relationship. Your partner needs to know what you will and won't tolerate (as you need to know what they will/won't put up with). If you never argue you never explore the boundaries of your relationship, and this is an important dance for lovers to do. However, there is a difference between thrashing out your differences in the Battle Zone and spending a lifetime there fighting over every single little issue.

Talk to Daniel and he can help you to pick your battles carefully using your Raphael List. The first five items on your list are the most important things to you. These are your non-negotiables. Let's say "honesty" is up there at number one—then if your partner lies to you they break your most important condition for the relationship. If "kindness" is number two and your partner is cruel, abusive, or hurtful, then condition number two has been broken. If "loyalty" is important to you, then any infidelity or betrayal breaks that condition, and so on. Any of these misdemeanors will send you into the Battle Zone to defend your beliefs. For the relationship to survive and thrive, these conditions have to be set and met on both sides by both of you.

Tip 1. If you want your partner to respect your conditions for a relationship, do not give them a long list where the important gets lost in the trivial. After all, you wouldn't be happy if they did it to you.

Love is like a *precious* plant. You've got to really look after it and *nurture* it.   JOHN LENNON

Tip 2. Do not set conditions that are unrealistic for the average human being to meet. If you tell a man that he cannot even look at another woman, or if you tell a woman that she can only buy one pair of shoes, you are heading straight for the Battle Zone without passing "Go."

Where you set your boundaries for the relationship is up to you, and everyone is different, but once you have set them, don't keep them a secret. Only angels are telepathic, so if you want your partner to respect your conditions you have to explain clearly what they are. One girl told me that she was devastated because her boyfriend had betrayed her trust by sending messages to other girls on the internet. However, he thought it was just a bit of harmless fun. She had never told him how she felt about chat rooms, so how could he know that he was upsetting her? Ignorance (in this case) is a valid defense. It is up to you to convey clearly what you will and won't tolerate in the relationship. This does not need to be a long, tedious process with hours of deep meaningful conversations about "us." Effective communication is about getting your message over succinctly and successfully. This is where Daniel's influence is invaluable. If you have a problem, he will guide you on how to broach the subject, get your point across, and bring the discussion to an end—just like a good business meeting.

Angel Advice

tips on how to be heard

1 Pick your time. Don't do it during the football game on TV.

2 Prepare in advance and be sure you are right.

3 Stay calm and keep eye contact.

4 Stick to the facts—don't be distracted or diverted.

5 Don't be abusive or personal.

6 Listen to what they have to say.

7 Give them time to think about what you have said.

There will be many points on which you can negotiate and find common ground. So what if they have size eleven feet, support the Giants, or play the bassoon loudly? You can live with it, and you may even come to celebrate it as being part of them. Accepting someone else's "little ways" is all part of loving someone.

Peggy "Years ago I met a wonderful man and we went for a weekend to a hotel together to celebrate my birthday. I noticed that he had packed a large, heavy gift into the trunk of his car and I couldn't wait to see what it was. On the night of my birthday he carried it with some difficulty into the hotel restaurant and there it sat under the table throughout the meal. Finally over coffee he brought it out and told me to open it. Inside the box was a large mixing bowl and four gallons of windshield wiper fluid. He was smiling from ear to ear as he explained that he knew how I liked to make cakes and keep my car clean. Twenty years later the memory of it still makes me smile, although since then I have never expected that man (who is now my husband) to buy or do anything romantic, and he never has. But that hasn't stopped us from having a good marriage and three children together."

Trust is the key foundation of any successful relationship, but trust takes time. To be able to trust, and to gain your partner's trust, ask Daniel to help you to:

 —Want it. Desiring something brings it to you.
 —Say it. Clear communication prevents many assumptions and
   misunderstandings.
 —Do it. Make sure your actions match your words.
 —Deserve it. It is not enough to demand trust, you have to earn it.
 —Praise it. Be grateful for any trust placed in you.
 —Treasure it. Treat your partner's trust with respect.
 —Wait for it. The longer you show you can be trusted, the more you will be.

> You come to love not by *finding* the
> perfect person, but by *seeing* an imperfect
> person perfectly.   SAM KEEN

You will eventually be able to trust your partner and they will trust you. This is a wonderful basis for a relationship to develop and flourish.

It is unlikely that you will meet someone who agrees to every one of your conditions. Instead, they may agree with your important issues but disagree on other things. If this is not good enough for you, then you are deliberately deciding that the relationship will fail. It is an old cliché, but for any relationship to succeed there needs to be compromise on both sides. If you refuse to compromise, then you are seeking failure. This may seem crazy. Surely you are looking for love, not looking for love to fail? But sometimes we can be unaware of our own self-sabotage. You can take Cupid's arrow and shoot yourself in the foot with it.

You may want love and yet fear being in love. After all, you could get hurt, make a fool of yourself, or lose control. There are plenty of convincing reasons that love is a bad idea. You may even have proof. If you grew up with parents who constantly fought, if you have had your heart broken, if friends or family have been through painful breakups, you will shy away from such a dangerous thing. If you admit to Daniel that you are afraid of being hurt, he can help to release negative emotions. His energy can heal all past hurts and pain that is associated with relationships and free you to experience love for what it really is—a joyous, uplifting affirmation of the best that being alive can offer.

Moira "As we go through life from day to day we ask ourselves, 'What is it all about?' It's about loving the one person in your life, the one who will complete your soul. It's about a hug in the dark, the first smile in the morning, the shared joke, the tears for each other's pain. It's their smell, their eyes, their voice. It's having their coat to protect you when going into battle. When you lay your head down at night, it's the safety of their body next to yours. Hold these things dear in your heart forever, for these are love. What a beautiful treasure."

Love really is great. That is why there are so many poems, books, stories, and songs written about it. If you are in love, never explain or apologize, accept it for the wondrous gift that it is, and live it to the full. You are blessed; you are happy; you are flying with angels.

Love is *everything* it's cracked up to be.

ERICA JONG

Chapter Nine

The Wrong One

If you have followed the gorgeous guidance sent to you from the angels, then you will have found someone whom you love and who loves you. Well done. You don't need to read the rest of this book and can skip straight to *The Angels' Guide to Marriage* for help with your "happy ever after." However, love never comes with a guarantee. You only have to look around at people you know, celebrity couples, and the divorce statistics to realize that not all relationships succeed. It's a depressing fact that the odds on a new romance succeeding are roughly 100:1. Love is such a risky business, but usually it's worth the gamble. If your romance floats into troubled waters, then you need the help of an angel who is a specialist in pouring oil on such situations. You need Raguel.

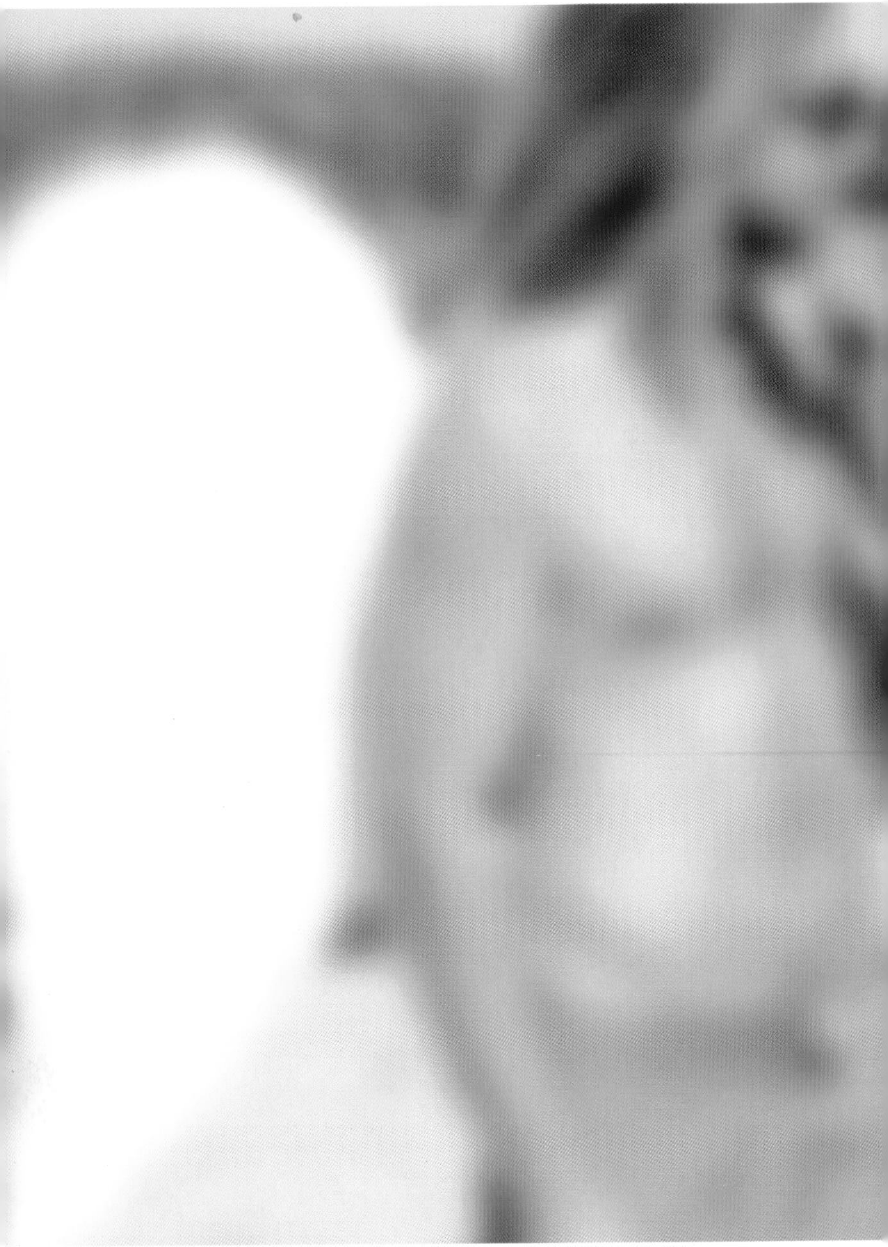

Archangel Raguel

The Mediator

The name Raguel means "Friend of God" and he
is often referred to as the "Angel of Justice."
Raguel is the angel who oversees disputes,
arguments, and trouble within relationships. This
is not an easy job. He works to resolve difficult
situations and to find answers to seemingly
impossible questions. He guides people to act in
fair and just ways and he reveals deception. His
energy is pale blue or aquamarine, so don't be
surprised if you are drawn to this color when he
is helping you.

A relationship is like a *rose*, how long it lasts,

no one *knows*.   ROB CELLA

Call upon Raguel's help whenever you feel that a dispute is beyond hope, and if there is a solution he will find it. Listen to your thoughts and feelings, especially the ones that won't go away. These so-called "gut" feelings are really messages from Raguel telling you what you need to know, even if you'd rather not know it. If you have ever suspected that something was wrong but you ignored your instincts, you refused to listen to Raguel. People are very good at blocking out any Raguel messages that they don't want to hear. This is why so many people are lied to, cheated on, and abused—because they refuse to admit what is happening to them, until it is too late and they have to deal with the consequences. The three common offenses that cause the most trouble are:

—Dishonesty.
—Infidelity.
—Abuse.

Any of these three can force someone to move directly from the Love Zone to the Retreat Zone and then exit the relationship. Asking Raguel to help you to deal with them will either save your relationship or give you the strength to end it.

Dishonesty. Dishonesty is not just telling lies; it is also manipulation, avoiding or being frugal with the truth, insincere emotions, and deceitful actions. The angels urge you to be honest, to build the blocks of trust that give your relationship a solid foundation. Dishonesty leaves it in ruins.

If you want the relationship to last, you need Raguel's help to be truthful. Most lies are created out of fear: Perhaps you are afraid that they will leave you if they know the truth, so one lie leads to another until truth is a stranger. You may tell yourself that you are protecting them by lying, but now you are lying to yourself, too. You are really trying to protect yourself, not them. There is no such thing as a white lie, only black secrets, and they cast dark shadows over your life together; things that can never be acknowledged but are always there. Often, the deception hurts more than the original secret, so you need to find the courage to tell the truth. Raguel will help you to release the fear of rejection that makes you deceitful. A romance based on lies never lasts and if you are dishonest you risk losing everything. You will be found out at some point and when that happens you may not get the chance to explain yourself or put things right. You may lose the very person that you claim to be protecting.

If you are being lied to, you may feel that ignorance is bliss. What you don't know can't hurt you, right? That is why so many people ignore Raguel's warning messages. They simply do not want to face something painful, so they get the shovels out and bury their heads in the sand, instead. This can go on for years and even lifetimes, with one person bluffing and the other one letting them get away with it. But ignorance is not bliss, it is just ignorance. It is a lack of knowledge about the truth. The truth may well be painful, it may pull the rug from under you and it may destroy your world. But ask yourself—which would you really rather do: live a lie or face the truth?

Angel Advice
lies lovers tell
And what they really mean

1 You are the first. *You are the nearest.*

2 I love you. *I want to sleep with you.*

3 I never fake ... *except when I'm tired, bored, etc.*

4 I don't fancy your friend. *Your friend doesn't fancy me.*

5 We are just good friends. *We haven't had sex—yet.*

6 It didn't mean anything. *I thought I'd get away with it.*

7 I need some space. *Bye bye.*

Angel Advice
signs that they are cheating

1 New underwear and a sudden interest in grooming.

2 Going AWOL.

3 Lack of appetite—they've already eaten.

4 Excess internet activity and cell phone calls.

5 Unexplained gifts for them.

6 Guilty gifts for you.

7 No sex or much better sex.

Infidelity. One of the most frequent reasons that people lie to their lover is because they have another lover tucked away somewhere. As we discovered in Chapter Seven, there are some people who cannot commit to an exclusive relationship, so they have two or more simultaneous romances. This usually necessitates a lot of fibbing, as most people are not thrilled by the idea of sharing their lover with someone else.

Men and women cheat for different reasons. The most common reason that women give for infidelity is "loneliness"; for men it's "opportunity." It seems that for women it is a deliberate act, considered in advance and in response to an emotional need, whereas for men it is a crime of chance. They can, so they do. That might explain why more married men (22 percent) than married women (14 percent) admit to having strayed at some time, although it may be that more women lie about it when asked.

It is unusual for someone who is happily in love (in the Love Zone) to start an affair. It is much more common for an infidelity to be a symptom rather than the disease. Usually, unresolved issues make someone unhappy, unloved, or unappreciated, until conditions are ripe for another love affair to start. If you are being unfaithful, ask yourself why. Raguel can help you identify what made you seek love elsewhere. Maybe you feel trapped, smothered, bullied, neglected, used, bored, scared, taken for granted, or mistreated. Whatever the reason (or combination of reasons), Raguel will reveal to you whether the next step is to enlist his help to work things through or ask him for the strength to end it.

If you are the unsuspecting partner of someone who is having an affair, Raguel can help you to realize what is going on. If you ask for his enlightenment, he will help you notice clues that you may normally overlook. Pay attention to any repetitive thoughts or annoying misgivings that keep popping into your mind. If you get an urge to do something but don't know why, always act on it. Open that letter, check that e-mail, answer that cell phone, wear that disguise and trail them down the street—well, okay, you can take things too far.

Not everyone is a player, so don't get paranoid, but do be careful. If Raguel opens you up to see evidence that you cannot ignore, you owe it to your own self-esteem to do something about it. If someone is disrespecting you, have enough respect for yourself to stop it happening.

Abuse. There is a common misconception that abuse means a black eye, but it can be much more subtle than that. Abuse can come in many different and equally sinister guises. There is verbal abuse, which includes disrespect, name calling, ridicule, derision, intimidation, and rudeness. There is emotional abuse, including withdrawal, coldness, refusal to communicate, anger, threats, blackmail, and terror. Then there is the easiest to spot, physical abuse, including violence, sexual abuse, and bullying. What an explicit list of horrible behavior that is. Sadly, you probably have (or will) come across at least one of these ways of behaving at some point in your dating adventures.

It is easier to *keep* half a dozen lovers guessing than to keep one lover after he has *stopped* guessing.   HELEN ROWLAND

How *empty* of me to be so *full* of you.

JANET JACKSON

Jenny "I don't feel the same way about my husband as I did when we were married, for many reasons. He always puts me down, he wants me to get a better job and make more money. I always wanted a family. We have no kids. I want them one day. Life just isn't good. My husband is controlling. When I clean the house, I must scrub the floors on my hands and knees. He won't let me bring home any fattening food so I won't get fat. God forbid if he sees me watching television. He yells at me, saying that I am lazy. I am not happy at all in my marriage. I just think it has been over for a long time."

See if any of this feels familiar...

- —You meet someone and they flatter you. They tell you that you are the most amazing person that they have ever met and that they will never meet anyone else like you. You have made them so very happy.
- —They make you feel special and "chosen" and you are told that no one else will give you the attention or adoration that they can give you.
- —They tell you that no one else could love you as much as they do and anyone who criticizes the relationship is jealous or doesn't understand. You start to do everything that you can to please them.
- —Then they start to criticize little things that you say or do. You try harder and make every effort to please them. They find fault with who you are, what you did in the past, and how you behave now. You become confused.
- —Any disagreements are blamed on you. It is your fault if you argue. It is your behavior that is wrong and unacceptable. If you would only do what they tell you to do, everything would be wonderful, like it used to be.
- —If you try to be independent they say that they are going to leave you.

his pattern of behavior is the recognized way that cult leaders "brainwash" their members into joining, staying, and sometimes dying for the cult. It is also the pattern of an abusive personal relationship. This is what is really going on:

- They flatter you to make you like them. They make you responsible for their happiness.
- They play on your insecurities and loneliness.
- They isolate you from your friends and family and other meaningful relationships.
- They become the focus of your thoughts and actions.
- They start to undermine your confidence and self-belief and they refuse to let you make them happy. They continue to undermine everything that you believe about yourself, as you don't understand how you could be so wonderful once and yet so worthless now. You lose sight of who you were and who you wanted to be.
- They create a climate of fear and make you believe that everything is your fault.
- They threaten to withdraw and make you lonely again, leaving you with the nothingness that they have created.

Raguel can open your eyes to an abusive relationship. He can reveal the ugly truth that you may have avoided in the past. If you are the abuser, you know you have to change. If you are being abused, you can change the situation. Both of you are responsible if it carries on.

If you love yourself you do not need to control, bully, or manipulate anybody else, and if you love yourself you will also not allow anyone else to control, manipulate, or bully you. The bottom line is that if your lover is nicer to the mailman than they are to you, take a good long look at what your so-called romance is all about. The only realistic choice you have in an abusive relationship is to walk away. As hard as it is, you need to get yourself, your pride, and your courage together and get the hell out.

Leanne "I used to live with a man who was violent. If he had a bad day at work he would come home and take it out on me. Even if nothing upset him he would still hit me just because he could. I never understood why he did it and always thought that one day he would change. We had a son together but that didn't change anything. One night when my baby was six months old my partner came home from a night out drinking. I knew what that meant so I locked myself in the bathroom. He ranted and raved and tried to kick the door down. I was terrified, but after a while he went away. When I came out I found him asleep on the sofa. I looked at him and felt nothing but disgust. I asked aloud, 'Why me? Why was I treated this way?'

"That's when I heard a voice in the back of my mind that I will never forget. It said, 'You can walk away any time that you like. It is your choice to stay.' It was like an angel was talking to me. I felt so stupid that I had never thought about leaving. That night I packed a bag, picked up my son, and left. I never went back."

As far as the angels are concerned, it all comes down to love. If you love someone you will not lie to them, cheat on them, or abuse them in any way. Their feelings are just as important as your own feelings are to you—or even more so. Consequently, you want to do your very best to make them happy. If it is only how you feel that matters to you, then you are not in love with anyone but yourself. Raguel is the great revealer. He can lovingly help you to face the facts and see the reality of any situation. This may be hurtful but, like lancing a carbuncle, the short-term pain will bring long-term gain. Trust that although conflict and change may be uncomfortable to go through, they will eventually lead to a better place. You do not have to live with that nagging feeling that something is not quite right; you can find out what it is, confront it, and move on to find greater peace in your life.

Chapter Ten

Losing that One

What on earth can angels do if your lover is a liar, a cheat, or a bully? This is not what you signed up for when you drew up your Raphael List, listened to Gabriel's messages, or took Uriel's advice. Surely this angel dating thing has gone horribly wrong? Not necessarily. As they say, what doesn't kill you makes you stronger. You may not feel very strong if you are curled up in the corner because you are disillusioned, betrayed, or bruised, and it is difficult to see a happy tomorrow if you are stuck in a miserable today, but all things pass with time and nothing stays the same. Things will get better. In the meantime you need an angel to hold you in his wings and bring you comfort—you need Zadkiel.

Archangel Zadkiel

The Releaser

Zadkiel means "Righteousness of God." He helps
people to release toxins from their hearts. He is
particularly effective at working with you when
you are asleep. If you ask him to visit you in
your dreams he will do so; when you wake up
you will be able to understand what is going on
and what you have to do. His energy works
through a deep indigo blue color, so don't be
surprised to see a lot of this shade when he is
influencing you.

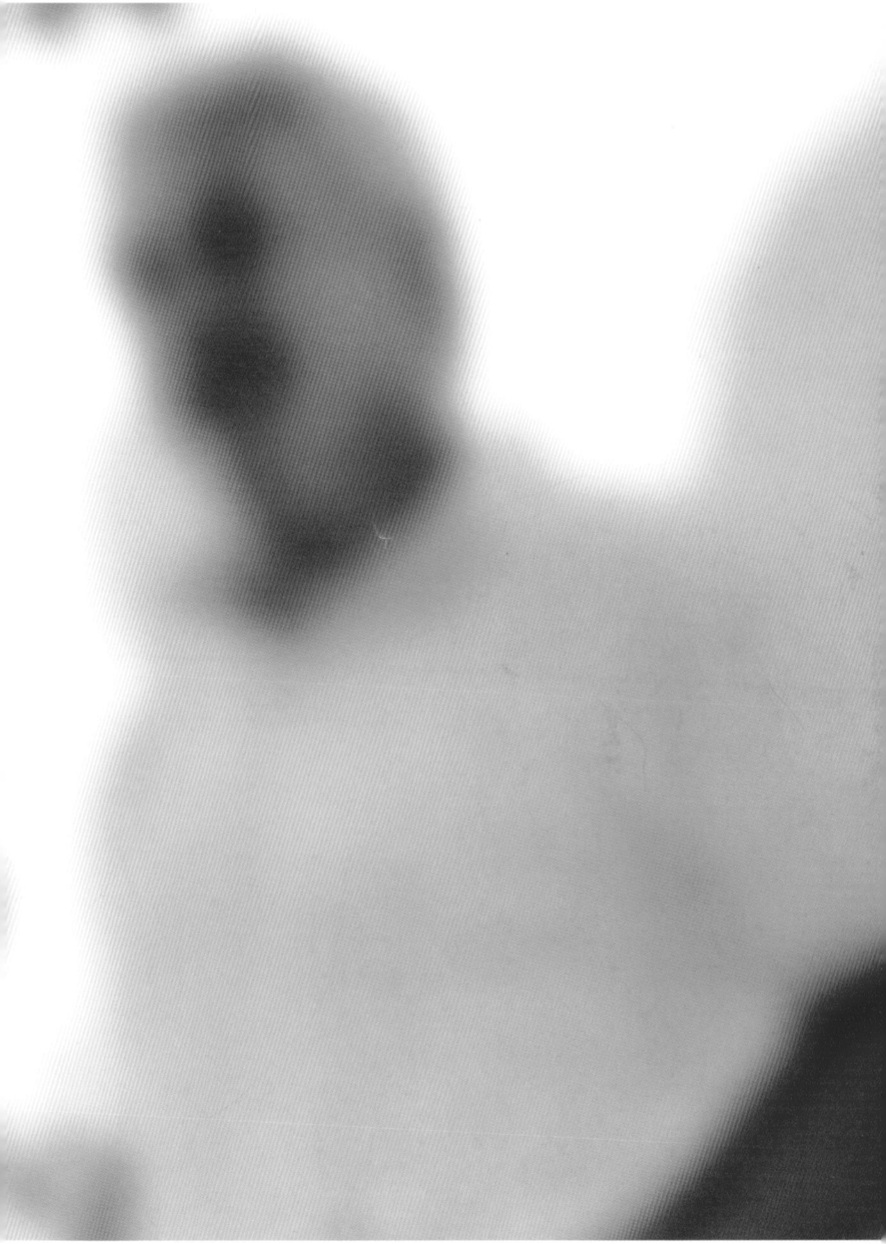

The *magic* of our first love is the *ignorance* that it can ever end.   BENJAMIN DISRAELI

In any confusing or emotionally fraught situation Zadkiel acts like a powerful cleaner, tidying up scattered and battered feelings. He will make you think more clearly so you can make decisions based on sound judgment rather than your (unpredictable) emotions. He will send you very definite guidance in the form of repetitive thoughts or feelings, or even in a more physical way through things you hear, see, or are told by others. However the messages come, you will not be able to ignore them, as they urge you to improve the situation for all involved.

Helen "Last Saturday I got this really strong feeling that I should look at my boyfriend's cell phone. I don't know why. I saw two text messages from some girl. I went cold and my legs went weak. One said that she missed him and the other said she couldn't wait to see him again. I confronted him, but he said they were only texts and I was overreacting. He made me feel like I had done something wrong. Every time his phone bleeps I am suspicious. He claims that she is a friend from years ago and that they have always kept in touch, but he never mentioned her before. Now I don't know what to think or whether to believe him or not. This uncertainty and feeling of doubt is tearing me up. How do I know if he is lying? How can I ever relax and feel safe again?"

A good relationship is built on mutual respect and trust, but trust is like a glass vase: perfect until broken, then almost impossible to put back together as it was. If the trust in your relationship has been shattered, you have three choices

—Stay and do nothing.
—Stay and try to mend it.
—Go.

Zadkiel will support you in whichever choice you make without judgment. The first option is totally up to you. Deciding to do nothing is accepting the situation as it is. Avoiding making a decision is the same thing. Your relationship will either improve or deteriorate, but you will have no influence over which way it goes. If you keep on doing what you've always done, you will keep on getting what you have always had. If you don't want to rock anyone's boat, then you live with that choice. Ask Zadkiel to lend you an arm to lean on as you go forward, and if you need more of his help he will gladly give it.

Often Zadkiel will act as a catalyst to bring the situation to a head in some way. There may be a great revelation, an argument, or an intervention by a third party. Once you have been confronted with the problem, Zadkiel then works with you to find a way through it. He is the best mediator in the universe, so if he can't find a solution to your problem then there isn't a solution to be found. He will send you guidance through thoughts, feelings, and intuition and he can also help you to release anger and find forgiveness. All you have to do is ask him to intervene and you will know in your heart whether you can work things out or whether this particular problem is the one that ends your relationship.

As the song says, "breaking up is hard to do." It can be equally unpleasant whether you are dumping someone or being dumped. All right, that's not strictly true, but it is not nice for anyone. Even if you are the one ending the romance you can have feelings of uncertainty, guilt, and remorse. You might have been driven to make this decision by your partner's actions or because you no longer feel the way you used to about them. Nevertheless, you probably have no desire to cause pain and distress. It's not nice being the bad guy and it is easier to be sinned against than sinning. What happens during a breakup is that both lovers go through the same process. It starts with uncertainty and moves through disillusion, discontent, and detachment until it arrives at disappearance. The dumper goes through the process first and the dumped can be left behind, unaware of what is going on, until they are forced to catch up. Whether you are cast as the villain or the victim of the splitting-up process, Zadkiel can help you.

Alice "Everyone thinks that when you leave someone you are a bad person, cruel and coldhearted, but it broke my heart to leave my husband. I didn't really want to break up the marriage but I had to. I had just reached the end of my ability to live with his lies. He wasn't a bad man, and I know that he loved me, but he used to lie about money. He even stole from our bank account to pay for things and then lied and said that he had been given them. I suppose he was just weak, but each time I found out, the same thing would happen. I would be shocked, then upset, then angry. He would be sorry, then contrite, but then he would go and do it again. Slowly I just lost all respect for him and, once that went, so did my love for him."

Villain. It may start with the tiniest inkling that something is not quite right: They said something wrong, their laugh began to get on your nerves, they broke a promise, upset your mum, kicked the cat, ate your last piece of chocolate, kissed your friend. Slowly, this undercurrent of doubt grows into a torrent of annoyance and becomes an ocean of certainty that things are very definitely wrong. But how do you know if it is really time to go? Try answering these seven Zadkiel questions:

- —Do I look forward to seeing him/her?
- —Do I make time for him/her?
- —Do I enjoy being with him/her?
- —Does he/she make me happy?
- —Does he/she make me proud?
- —Do I trust him/her?
- —Do I see a future with him/her?

If your answer is "No" to any of these, you are in trouble, and so is the relationship. Zadkiel will give you the extra understanding that you need to make the decision to end it. Once you know this, please act on it. Don't just hope that it will happen all by itself. Avoiding them, behaving badly, or sleeping with their best friend are not angelic ways of letting them know that it's over.

or whatever they once meant to you (and you must have liked them once or you wouldn't be in this mess now) you owe it to them to end this relationship fairly.

This is a job for Zadkiel, who will give you the courage and protection that you need to break away and find a new life, and the compassion to do it kindly. He will instruct you where and when to do it. As a rule of thumb, you don't want an audience but you do want an exit that either of you can use. Do not hope that your soon-to-be ex will understand or agree with you. One day they may, given time and healing, but right now emotions are too raw. Also, don't look for sympathy from anyone, even if you had no choice. If you have been on the receiving end of bad behavior such as lies, abuse, or betrayal, you may get the chance to explain your reasons to some close friends, who may or may not understand. The important thing is that you fully understand your motivation for finishing this relationship.

Angel Advice
bad ways to dump someone

1 In front of their friends.

2 Using any kind of microphone.

3 In bed.

4 Writing it in their Valentine's card.

5 By text, e-mail, fax, or on a website.

6 During any Tom Hanks and/or Meg Ryan film.

7 Jokingly ... "Guess who just split up— we did."

Friendship often *ends* in love,

but love in friendship—*never*.

CHARLES CALEB COLTON

Zadkiel's

"Don'ts of dumping"

—Don't hang around. If you are sure, then do it
sooner rather than later.
—Don't give hints hoping to soften the blow.
They will be left in a torment of wondering
and waiting, which is not fair.
—Don't tell anyone else first. Your soon-to-be ex
deserves to hear it from you and no one else.
—Don't give mixed signals. Being affectionate or
complimentary will confuse the message.
—Don't waffle or go off on a tangent. This is
important news, so deliver it straight.
—Don't be aggressive, get personal, or apportion
blame.
—Don't give false hope or use the "we can still
be friends" line—you can't.

"Do's of dumping"

—Do be prepared and clear about what you want
to say.
—Do pick a good time and place.
—Do be sincere and honest about your reasons.
—Do keep it to a time limit to stop it dragging
on for hours.
—Do listen to what they have to say. They have
the right of reply.
—Do leave alone.
—Do give yourself time and space to let go.

an "I had been thinking about asking Sandy to marry me for a few months, but every time I mentioned our future together she would go all vague and change the subject. I figured the only thing to do was to take the plunge and propose, so she knew how serious I was about her. I spent ages choosing the ring, even though I couldn't afford it. I was so nervous that I drank a little too much during dinner, but afterward I went down on one knee and did the whole thing properly. The restaurant came to a standstill waiting for her answer but she thought I was joking. It was when I pulled out the ring box from my pocket that I knew I had made a big mistake. Her face was like thunder and she got up and left. It was like a bad scene from a film. The next day when I got back from work she had gone. She cleared out all her stuff and just left. I was devastated and tried to get her on the phone but she wouldn't talk to me. One day I was happily planning a life with her, the next day she was out of my life completely. I heard from friends that she had moved out of town, but I don't know any more than that. I thought we were happy together."

Zadkiel makes you realize that you have been in an abusive relationship, you can end it knowing that you are about to regain everything that you had lost. It is extraordinary how fast you reclaim your own power if you take it back from someone who has been using it against you. They are left powerless, and even if they beg you to come back, do not fall for it. They may say that they are sorry, that they cannot live without you, and they may break down in tears. Sadly, they are not crying for you but for themselves. They are about to lose the identity that being a bully gave them, the superiority that your inferiority supplied. Well, tough. Think about it. If you were really so stupid, ugly, fat, and pathetic (or whatever other insults they threw at you) why would they want you back? The minute you are on the other side of the door you will begin to feel better and they will begin to learn the right way to treat people.

Angel Advice

things not to do after you've been dumped

1 Start a candlelit vigil outside their house.

2 Burn their house down.

3 Put naked pictures of them on the internet.

4 Drink the nearest bar dry.

5 Jump under a bus or push them under one.

6 Sleep with their best friend.

7 Book yourself into the nearest convent/monastery.

Victim. It may start with the tiniest inkling that something is not quite right: they looked at you a certain way, ignored you, avoided your calls, wouldn't hug you, picked a fight, made you cry, rolled their eyes at everything you said, kissed your friend. Or it may come like a bolt of lightning—your lover has called it a day.

If you are relieved or even pleased with this news, then you probably don't need Zadkiel's help, but if it is the one thing that you feared most, you definitely do.

People can do the most extraordinary things after the "It's over" conversation, things that they would never conceive of doing at any other time. Powerful emotions—such as shock, embarrassment, disappointment, shame, anger—all jumbled up together, can lead to some pretty irrational behavior. A bit like the madness of infatuation, you may be forgiven for anything that you do during the immediate period following a breakup. It may be forgiven, but not forgotten. In order to prevent you from doing or saying anything that you may regret later, ask Zadkiel to intervene.

Every *heartache* carries with it the *seed* of an equal or greater benefit.   NAPOLEON HILL

"Do's of being dumped"

–Do understand that you are in shock.

–Do recognize your pain as a valid emotion.

–Do get support from friends.

–Do be kind to yourself and do whatever you
  need to do to feel better.

–Do give it time. You need to grieve and heal.

–Do look to the future, when you won't feel
  like this.

–Do try to see it as an opportunity, not a crisis.

"Don'ts of being dumped"

–Don't see it as failure.

–Don't manipulate or threaten repercussions.

–Don't take your hurt out on anyone or
  anything else.

–Don't bring up past grievances to use as
  weapons.

–Don't try to argue or change their mind; you
  won't be able to.

–Don't lose your dignity, integrity, or self-
  respect. Nobody is worth that.

–Don't think that this is the end for you and
  romance–it isn't.

You will need help in the first couple of days, in particular, as these are the hardest. It is okay to scream, blubber till there are no more tears, and eat a mountain of carbohydrates. A good friend may lend you vital support at this time, but if you don't want a witness to your misery you can send out an emergency S.O.S. and, along with Zadkiel, hundreds of other angels will gather around to soothe and console you.

If you need a session of comfort eating then call in the **Chocolate Angels**. *These angels oversee the manufacture of all types of chocolate—which sounds like a great job to me. They will manifest bars of the magical brown stuff at the back of cupboards, down the sides of sofas, and at the bottom of bags, so that you will always find one when you need a sugar boost.*

Whatever you need to do, give yourself permission to do it. Anything that boosts your confidence again is allowed at this point, so do something nice for yourself: Give yourself a treat, have a massage, get a new look, go to your favorite place/park/café, and hang out with people who will refill your depleted reservoir of self-esteem. There are just two important exceptions to this "whatever gets you through" philosophy.

First no-no. Do not have any contact with your now ex. Do not call, text, e-mail, "accidentally" bump into them, or deliberately go around to see them. If necessary, give your cell phone to a friend so that you won't be tempted in a weak moment. Have a "panic buddy" ready to whom you can talk, or ask Zadkiel to put a block on any self-destructive actions. You need to amputate, and the last thing you need is a reminder of just how painful that operation is.

Tiny "I thought I'd handled the breakup really well. After she told me, I walked away with a small amount of dignity and I even managed a weak smile and what I hoped was an 'it's your loss' look. The next weekend I got absolutely hammered and phoned her in the early hours of Sunday morning. As it was happening I knew it was a bad idea, but her number was in my cell phone and I was out of control. I don't know what I said, but apparently it was a mixture of calling her a slut and begging her to take me back. I didn't even know I had done it until two days later, when she called me to see if I was okay. It makes me squirm now just to think about it."

Remember the way that angels manipulate electrical devices? If you ask the **Telephone Angels** *to be on your side they will block any calls that you are tempted to make in a weak moment. If you punch in your ex's number at two in the morning after three bottles you will be saved from connecting. The* **Telephone Angels** *will intervene in some way, even erasing any embarrassing message that you leave, so that you are spared that "Oh no, what did I do?" feeling the morning after.*

Second no-no. Whether you are the villain or the victim, whether you decided to dump or you were dumped on, whether you are ready to move on or you are stuck temporarily with no concept of what happens next, there is one thing to avoid at all costs. Never, ever, have sex with an ex. There are too many strong feelings and confusing emotions involved. Does this mean they still like me? Is the romance back on? Can we make a go of it again? Even if you tell yourself it is just physical and doesn't mean anything, it is not and it does. It is more than just a release of bodily tension; it is an act of intimacy that promises more. It is a minefield of feelings that can lead to false hopes, misuse of power, and more disappointment and heartache. If it's over, it is over.

By the time a partnership *dissolves*, it has *dissolved*.   JOHN UPDIKE

Linda "I was a housewife and mother. After twenty years of marriage my husband left me and my world fell apart. It's hard to describe what it's like when everything suddenly crumbles away. My sons had their own friends and their own lives were just beginning, but I was thirty-nine and my whole life revolved around my husband. Money was tight and I had to get a job, so I started to work part-time in a big furniture store and began to make friends there. Soon, I actually started to enjoy my new freedom. I told the boys that they had to do their own washing from now on, as I was too busy with my own life. I saw that I had been trapped all my life. I had been a willing slave to three men. Now, my life is totally different. I even look different. I feel much more like me—the 'me' that I should always have been. Isn't it funny how things work out?"

One thing that Zadkiel and all the angels excel at is turning a negative into a positive. That's what angels do. They take bad things and make them better. In this instance, what seems like an ending is really the beginning of something new. Zadkiel can help you to change the way you view things and heal your aching heart. With Zadkiel's help you will be able to release the past, see a future, and even start to plan ahead.

Chapter Eleven

Table for One

Loss is an inevitable part of love. Unless you met your lover at grade school and you both die at exactly the same time, in an accident or a suicide pact, one of you will experience the loss of the other at some time. So get used to the idea. You live knowing that you will die, and you love knowing that you will lose. The inevitability of one does not stop the other from happening. Your romance may have ended but your life hasn't. This is when you need to have a friend like Azrael.

Archangel Azrael

The Counselor

Azrael's name means "Whom God helps" and he is known as the "Angel of Death." In this respect he has always had a bad press, as he is portrayed as a sickle-wielding dark demon. In reality, he couldn't be less like that. He is the softest, kindest, gentlest angel—one of his main duties is to comfort people when they die. He lovingly surrounds their spirit as it makes its transition from one world to another. His kindness and compassion is beyond measure, so he is the angel who can comfort you during any difficult transition in your life. He can ease your troubled mind and soul and even help you to sleep better. Azrael's energy is a soft cream color, so you may see more of this when he is around.

At the beginning and at the end of *love*, the two lovers are *embarrassed* to find themselves alone.

JEAN DE LA BRUYÈRE

The pain of lost love is almost physical. You feel it like a lead weight in your stomach and your heart. You cannot see a future and, even if you could, you haven't got the energy to face it. But stop for just a moment. Notice anything? You are still breathing, the birds are still singing, the world is still turning, and life goes on, so you had better decide what you are going to do with it. Things have changed and there is no going back. But before you can move forward you must grapple with the grieving process, which sounds like a job for Azrael.

Azrael is the angel who heals broken hearts. How long this takes depends on what kind of person you are, what happened, and how deeply you were involved in the first place. This is not necessarily about how long you were in the relationship—it is possible to fall far and fast—but as a general rule, the longer you have been in love, the harder it is to climb out of it. Some people are astoundingly resilient and bounce back from heartbreak determined to give it another go. But most of us need time to adjust and move from one circumstance to the next. If you are prepared to give your body time to recover from a physical wound, then you must be prepared to give your heart time to recover from being broken. Again there are no "rules" about how this process happens, but there are seven stages that you will go through; Azrael can hold your hand every step of the way.

One silver lining at the end of a relationship is the "Been Dumped Diet." It is an unusual phenomenon whereby people who have been recently dumped often lose a lot of weight very quickly. It could be due to appetite loss but even if you eat a quart tub of ice cream every night, you will find you still shrink by at least fifteen pounds. Think of it as the angels' way of compensating you for going through such a nasty experience.

Shock. The first step is about survival. You wake up, you breathe, you might eat, you don't sleep, you sometimes forget that everything has changed until it hits you again like another blow to your chest. You welcome numbness and may seek it at the bottom of a glass or in another pair of arms—anything is better than the jolt of realization that you are not part of a couple anymore. You will not be able to concentrate on much, so, if possible, take time off work or tell a few close colleagues what is going on so that they can cover for you. You may become preoccupied and careless, so watch out for mishaps or accidents. One friend of mine was so distracted after her husband left her that she forgot to brake and slammed into the back of a police car.

Azrael will protect you in many ways at this time. You may have to move home, change locks, rearrange finances, cancel credit cards, or decide who gets what. You will not feel like doing any of these things, but they are necessary so Azrael will push you to do them. He will be watching out for your self-interest and making sure that you focus on important matters and make the necessary adjustments to insure your well-being.

Angel Advice
things women say after being dumped
things men say after being dumped

1 We'll get back together. *I never liked her anyway.*

2 It's my fault. *It's all her fault.*

3 Nobody will ever love me. *Plenty more fish.*

4 I'll never trust anyone again. *She'll be sorry.*

5 Why? *Whatever.*

6 All men are bastards. *All women are evil.*

7 I want him back. *I want someone with bigger breasts.*

Denial. When the shock wears off it may be replaced by denial. You don't want what is happening to happen, so you will tell yourself that it is not happening. Simple. It is just a hiccup, a blip, another argument, they will come round and things will be just like they used to be. Wrong. Your partner is now your ex-partner and the sooner you confront that reality, the sooner you can begin the healing process. Azrael will come to you in your quiet times, particularly when you are asleep, and help you to understand that the relationship is over. If you wake up and your first conscious thought is about your partner and what has happened, then Azrael has been with you in the night, gently urging you to accept the change in your life.

Anger. The next stage is ugly. You become mad as hell. How can they treat you like this? After all you've been through, all you did for them and all you meant to each other. You are not about to be tossed aside like an old rag. You'll show them.

Please don't. You are not in control of this situation, or of yourself, at this time so, no matter what they did, please do not plot your revenge. While it may give you temporary satisfaction to rip up their clothes, pour their wine down the drain, or slash their tires, in the long run this will only make you feel worse. Everyone knows that you are hurting, but how you handle that hurt is important for your pride. After all, haven't they done enough to you without taking away your dignity, too? Revenge is undignified and unnecessary.

Gilly "A fortnight after my ten-year relationship ended I saw a girlfriend for lunch. After a few pleasantries she asked how I was and that opened the floodgates. I ranted and raved against my ex and she listened politely. Then she pulled a book out of her bag and pushed it across the table.

Live well, it is the *greatest revenge*.
THE TALMUD

It was *The Girls' Guide to Surviving a Breakup* with a stupid cartoon on the front. She said it was time for me to 'pull myself together' and then she smiled at me with a sad look on her face. I wanted to shove that book right down her throat. It had been two weeks. Two weeks. Ten years of being with someone and I'm meant to get over it in two weeks. She still had her boyfriend, so she could be smug, her world hadn't been turned upside down. I told myself that she meant well, but it was clear that she had no idea what I was going through. I didn't want to 'get over it'; I was so angry that I wanted to kill someone."

Sadness. Anger usually gives way to sadness. Great rolling waves of misery that wash over you at the strangest of times: when you are in the bathroom, filling up your car with gas, or at the store. Something triggers a memory—a smell, a flower, a song—and suddenly you are engulfed in a black fog of misery and are weeping buckets. Your pockets are full of soggy Kleenex and you feel permanently red-eyed and drained. Be prepared for certain dates to slap you in the face. Anniversaries and birthdays will come around and be painful because your lover is not there to share them with you like they were last year. This is a normal phase of mourning your loss. It is a recognition that you loved and were loved and that this has ended. It is okay to be sad. Do not dismiss this as "wimpy" or pathetic. It is necessary to feel this grief in order to move beyond it. If you don't give due credence to this part of the process, it will only slow down your healing. This, more than any other time, is when you need Azrael's infinite care. If you ask, he will hold you in his wings in a loving embrace until you feel the anguish subside, replaced by his warm solace.

Loneliness. Following the turmoil of sadness comes the gaping hole of loneliness. The house is empty, the bed is empty, and you are empty. You have time on your hands, time that you used to spend together, so fill the extra hours with "stuff." Make yourself busy. Work like a maniac if you want, take up pottery, potholing, or write a potboiler. Get a potbellied pig. Do something that you always wanted to do but couldn't when you were with your ex. Do not

Angel Advice
things that make you feel better

1 Tell yourself that you will be fine.

2 Play rock music really loud and sing along.

3 Go outdoors and feel the force of nature.

4 Throw out junk and clear your space.

5 Practice smiling—even if you don't feel like it.

6 Do something daring—make yourself feel something other than sad.

7 Scream. It is a great release.

resent the excess time—celebrate it as freedom to explore new interests, new adventures, and new people. Call up friends and family and make arrangements to see them so that you have events to look forward to and a full calendar, especially at weekends. As well as preventing those long evenings of self-absorbed pity, it will give you a huge sense of pride to do something new and do it well. Be selective about who you spend time with at this point. Avoid negative people or those who either can't or won't understand. Choose to share yourself with only those who are genuinely on your side and rooting for your recovery. Family are fine, as they are always on your side—that is why they hide the photos of your ex. Mutual friends can be tricky. Usually they have to take sides and they will do this based on these criteria: Which of you did they know first, which of you do they feel closest to, and which of you do they consider responsible for the breakup? This is where the effort you made cultivating true friends will have really paid off. They will be on "your side" and form a shield around you until you feel stronger. They will listen when you need to talk, understand when you just want to be sad, and never mention the fact that they saw it coming.

Mark "My wife left me after fifteen years of marriage. I became very lonely as all my friends had families, and no one wants a single man hanging around like a spare part. I very quickly lost my self-esteem and I felt inadequate and a failure. I tried a dating agency, but it wasn't for me. I made some connections through the internet, but they were unfulfilling compared with the closeness of my relationship with my wife. There was no one I could talk to who was in the same situation as me."

Acceptance. Gradually you will find ways to take it on the chin. With Azrael's help, support from close allies, and time, you will slowly become resigned to life without your ex (get used to thinking of them as that). At some point you will feel like cleansing your world of things that remind you of them. Go through the CD collection, sort out the photographs, remove any old shoes or underwear that still linger in your closets, and store away any cards, jewelry or gifts that remind you of happier times. Resist the temptation to be dramatic and throw it all in the river. You probably won't believe this right now but there will come a time when you will appreciate having some mementos of them and, besides, there's sentimentality and there's stupidity. No matter how much they hurt you, at least sell their gifts and get a good price. One of my friends made a considerable sum selling all her ex's gifts on eBay.

Cleansing is a wonderful way to begin to claw back your confidence, power, and pride. Many people redecorate the house, buy a new wardrobe of clothes, or get a new hairstyle, without realizing that it is Azrael's healing influence that is making them do it. Your self-esteem may have walked out of the door right behind your partner, but this doesn't mean that it won't return. Unlike your ex, it hasn't gone forever, and you are in control of how you get it back.

Self-esteem is what it says on the can—it means holding yourself in high regard. Some people have no trouble with this and always think that they are wonderful, no matter how many knocks they take or mistakes they make. But for most of us self-esteem is an unpredictable companion. If things are going well, you ride high on the crest of your wonderfulness, but one little incident can bring you crashing to earth in a puddle of self-doubt. The angels always hold you in high regard, no matter what happens, so if you need an injection of admiration just call on Azrael to pick you up and set you back on your feet.

Angel Advice

reasons you are better off without him

1 No more endless hours of sport/ computer games.

2 You don't have to nurse him when he has "man flu."

3 Much less mess.

4 No more underpants on the floor or smelly feet.

5 Toilet seat stays where it should.

6 You can get real workmen around to do the jobs.

7 You can look at other guys.

He will pour positive, self-affirming thoughts into your mind until you begin to see yourself and your world in a more loving way. Something strange may start to happen at this point. You may realize that you are changing, or have changed, and you will probably like the new you. It comes as a pleasant surprise to realize that you are going to be okay.

Release. It is up to you whether you let go of the relationship or cling on to a sinking ship by your fingernails. Azrael has the power to make you release pain and resentment toward your ex and if you can do this you will free yourself of the heavy burden of regret. If you ask him, he will find forgiveness in your heart and provide the courage for you to set yourself free from the past. Once you get rid of those bad feelings you will create a void into which only good feelings can come. In other words, you will never have room in your heart for anything new until you empty it of the old. For a positive release, with help and support from Azrael, try the Releasing Ritual on the following pages.

We shall find *peac*

Patricia "My husband left me for another woman and I was devastated. I thought we had the perfect marriage, so when it happened to me I was embarrassed as well as shocked, hurt, and angry. As a matter of fact, I was furious. I wished he was dead and I damned him to hell. One night I made a complete fool of myself at a party and the following morning I decided to change. I decided it was time to move forward with my life and stop being so angry. I can't say that I forgave him until many years later. One day I was having dinner with some friends when one of them said that my ex and his new wife were emigrating to Australia and, before I knew what was coming out of my mouth, I said, 'Good luck to them.' Everyone looked at me in surprise. I think they expected me to wish that the plane would crash. The thing is that I really meant it. I no longer cared what he was doing and I wished him nothing but happiness. When I got home that night I realized that I had at some point finally let him go. I felt so relieved that I didn't have to carry around all that bad feeling anymore."

Angel Advice

reasons you are better off without her

1 No more endless hours of soaps.

2 Steak is back on the menu.

3 Lower telephone bills.

4 Razor stays where it should.

5 No more nagging.

6 The drain in the shower is not blocked with hair.

7 You can look at other girls.

shall hear *angels*.

ANTON CHEKHOV

Releasing Ritual

If, like me, you're not really into "mumbo jumbo" you may consider this to be a bit weird. I know I did, until I tried it and it really worked. The proof of the pudding ... If you are having a hard time letting go of your finished romance, if the memories are too painful, or if you can't shake the unhappiness, try this symbolic ritual:

Get together a candle, a photograph of your ex, a shoebox (or similar), some tape, some items that still have a sentimental meaning to you with regard to the relationship, and a small angel doll or figurine.

Light the candle and tell Azrael that you are ready to release all the feelings about your ex (good and bad) that you are still carrying around. Sit quietly and allow Azrael's energy to lift the emotion from you. Then put the sentimental items in the box and seal it with the tape. As you do, affirm that your ex was an important part of your life and mentally thank them for the time that you spent together.

Take the photograph and carefully burn it in the candle flame, telling Azrael that you are willing to let go of anything that is keeping you attached to your ex and the relationship that you had with them. Sit quietly. You will feel an amazing relief and lightness enter your body.

Take the angel doll and put all your trust in this symbol of hope for the future. Carry it around in your pocket and talk to it whenever you need strength or courage. If one of those black, miserable thoughts creeps up on you, take out the doll and hold it in your hands until you feel better.

Put the box somewhere out of sight, in the attic or a cupboard. (One of my clients buried hers in the garden and planted an azalea bush on top of it. Every time she looked at the flowers she smiled at how far she had come since that dark day.) Then thank Azrael for his empathy, his compassion, and his friendship. Trust me, you will feel healed.

This is a pretty personal ceremony so you will probably want to do it alone, but if you do invite a close friend to be a witness, the healing power will double. Then after the ritual is complete, make sure you have a party and celebrate your newfound freedom.

At this point you may feel like reaching out to new friends. Azrael will bring them into your sphere when you are ready to meet them. These people didn't know you when you were part of a couple, so they accept you for who you are and not to whom you were attached. As well as avoiding any painful conversations, new friends bring new energy and hope into your life. You may discover to your surprise (shock, horror) that you are still attractive to the opposite sex (or your own sex if that's your thing). You may even find yourself flirting again.

There's no way of predicting how long it will take to move through the seven stages of recovery from a broken heart. You might speed through them all in one day, or it could take weeks, months, or even years. You will still think of your ex, but that intense shooting pain will be replaced by a dull ache of regret. You will feel "normal" again and possibly even content. You may be starting to wonder what life has in store for you next. You become aware that if you can survive having your heart broken you can survive almost anything and you will be proud of yourself. Endings are also beginnings, so someone, somewhere, is waiting to meet you and they could be ten times better than the one you lost.

Chapter Twelve

Another One

"Will I get over it?" This annoying little question is what I ask myself whenever something bad happens, from a broken washing machine to a dead pet. It is a reality check. Something that seems important now will be trivial in a year's time. So next time life deals you a disappointment, annoyance, gripe, or even disaster, ask yourself, "Will I get over it?" The answer is usually "Yes" (unless it is a major trauma like a death, in which case you do learn to live with it). If you are suffering from a broken heart, ask yourself the same question: "Will I get over it?" The world is full of people who have been through heartbreak and who have survived, if not thrived, and lived to love again.

Archangel Jeremial

The Reviewer

Jeremial means "The Mercy of God" and his
energy works through a deep scarlet, almost
violet color. One of his jobs is to take over from
Azrael in the care of spirits when they pass over.
He helps them to review their lives and assess
what they got right and what they got wrong.
This is never done in a judgmental way (you do
not get scored on it) but instead in a loving,
compassionate environment where you can learn
the most. Fortunately you don't have to be dead
to benefit from Jeremial's wisdom. He can help
you to review any aspect of your life at any time.

If grass can *grow* through *cement*, love can find you at *every* time in your life.   CHER

Different people react in different ways to the end of a love affair. Some are "once bitten twice shy," while others don't know the meaning of the word "shy." Which of these sounds like you?

—I will never ever date again.
—I am going to date again immediately.
—I will date again when I am good and ready.

"That's it. I'm finished with dating. Give me a dog any day—they are loyal, do what you tell them to, and keep you warmer in bed." If everyone thought like this the human race would die out. It is only natural to be cautious after a bad experience, but it is not good to let it color the rest of your life. No one is saying that being deceived, betrayed, disappointed, or hurt is fun, but if you can move beyond these feelings and learn from them, you will have the courage to love again.

Diana "I thought that time would make me feel better; that if I just waited long enough the ache in my heart would go away. But as the months went by I was still missing him and wanting him back. I realized that I needed help. It was as if I was stuck and couldn't move past him, even though he was getting on with his life. Then, one day, I felt everything just lift off me. I can't explain it. I just got fed up with feeling that way and I asked out loud if I could just feel better. It was like a physical change; I felt lighter, more carefree; I remember almost skipping down the road with a big grin on my face. I am sure someone or something heard me and took away my pain."

Sometimes troubles are really answered prayers in disguise, so maybe, just maybe, the end of a relationship could be a good thing. The angel who is renowned for changing bad into good is Jeremial. He can help you to appreciate that what you have been through has made you stronger. He can prevent bitterness growing in your heart by opening it up to new experiences. He can help you to let go of blame or guilt and stop thinking of yourself as a victim. He will keep you positive. If you jumped off the dating cliff and got bruised by the fall, then Jeremial can patch you up again.

Some people get stuck in their unhappiness. As strange as it may seem, being unhappy has its advantages: You can get attention, sympathy, and free drinks. Sadness becomes the norm and then it becomes a warm, comfortable place to stay. I call these people the "woe is me" brigade, because they are never happier than when they are telling you how miserable they are. They are Olympic-Class Drains.

You may know somebody who has slipped into the "woe is me" category following a bad love affair, or (let's be honest) it might be you. If sadness has become a bit of a habit, it is time for Jeremial to help you to break it. Happiness is a choice and deciding that you will no longer be miserable is a conscious decision. See yourself as Jeremial sees you. Just for a moment use your imagination and pretend that you are an angel looking at yourself.

Angel Advice
signs that you have got over it

1 You don't cry when you hear "your song."

2 You stop plotting ways to make them suffer.

3 You return to places where you used to go together.

4 You stop reading their horoscope.

5 You smile at the mention of their name.

6 You wouldn't take them back.

7 You bless them and wish them happiness.

What do you see? Don't try too hard, just let the angels show you how they see you. You are a perfect human being with fire, spirit, and unlimited ability for happiness. Let Jeremial help you to tap into those reservoirs of joy and make you whole again. No other person can touch your inner spirit—it is a gift that is yours and yours alone. Give yourself permission to smile, thank, sing, skip, play, dance, giggle, and love again.

Being too anxious to date again is almost as problematical as being too reluctant. Some people choose to pick themselves up, climb to the top of the dating cliff, and throw themselves straight off again. Without spending time to heal, they grab the nearest likely candidate and plunge right in, thinking "this time it's love." You may know someone who gets knocked down romantically and gets up and carries on again like a character in a video game. This is disposable dating. If something breaks, throw it away and get a new one. But you only ever get one heart, so if that gets broken you need to give it time to mend. An open romantic wound will not heal without time and care. And yet so many people throw themselves into the next romantic adventure without taking the time to find out why the last one didn't work out. There are various types of serial daters. See if any of these seems familiar.

The Desperate Dater is never, ever single. They always have someone on their arm and in their bed, and their partners change with alarming regularity. It is very hard to keep up as they leapfrog from one romantic encounter to the next. They don't let themselves get too emotionally involved, so people never get too close to them. They distance themselves to avoid hurt, but often it makes their partner give up trying and leave. Their reaction to being dumped is to find a new lover as quickly as possible (and they usually have a few likely candidates lined up just in case).

The Delusional Dater. Hope springs eternal as they are always convinced that this new love is "the one." They fall far and fast and invest so much emotion so quickly that they scare people off. They assume that because they are experiencing all these wonderful feelings, the other person is too; they are booking the honeymoon before they have exchanged phone numbers. If their lover runs away they plunge into a trough of self-pity for a short time, before repeating the whole process with the next suitable target that comes into their sights.

The Defeatist Dater sets out on each new romance with the absolute conviction that it will never work out. They quote divorce statistics on the first date and it's not long before their self-fulfilling prophecy comes true. In the meantime they invest more emotion than they admit in the relationship, but they don't show this. Unaware of their true feelings and only told that it probably won't go anywhere, the partner becomes discouraged and moves on. Then the defeatist comes into their own as they revel in the "I told you so." They get a masochistic satisfaction from being right all along, without realizing that they caused the very thing that they predicted.

The Dangerous Dater is out to cause as much trouble to as many people as possible. Usually the root of their mischievousness lies in a broken heart. Someone hurt them in the past and, boy, is everyone else going to suffer for it now. At first they appear to be very keen and very involved in the relationship, but they are really just biding their time until they can start confusing, worrying, and upsetting their unsuspecting partner. They blow hot and cold, they manipulate and play mind games, and they get malicious enjoyment from it. The lover hangs in there as long as possible but eventually ejects from the relationship as an emotional wreck. This is a job well done for the dangerous dater who then turns their attention to the next victim.

Have you ever *dated* someone because you were *too lazy* to commit suicide?   JUDY TENUTA

The Dissatisfied Dater has impossibly high standards. Nobody will ever be good enough, rich enough, attractive enough, or intelligent enough for them. They don't date, they audition people and invite them to prove that they qualify for a little of their attention. It doesn't matter if the high opinion they have of themselves is not backed up, they still expect their date to be unreasonably wonderful. To them a lover is a status symbol reflecting their own shining wonderfulness. They don't get too emotionally involved as they are too busy loving themselves. If they do find someone who qualifies as a partner, he or she doesn't last long—one step out of line and they are history.

The Dedicated Dater makes a career out of dating. Nothing else—just dating. Their whole life revolves around the next object of their affections. They search for someone who exactly fits their ideal of what a partner should be, then they plan each encounter with military precision down to the last detail. They are never spontaneous. They become deeply uncomfortable if a lover fails to stick to the plan or (heaven forbid) has their own ideas about what should happen. Partners find their rigid rules hard to live with and, when dumped, the dedicated dater is extremely disappointed—not because they have lost a love but because their plan went wrong.

The Delinquent Dater hasn't got a clue what is going on. They live in a blissful bubble of ignorance, bouncing from one romance to another without really understanding anything. They are totally unaware of the emotional fallout that they leave behind because they are incapable of understanding their own feelings, never mind anyone else's. They are not deliberately malicious—they are just oblivious to almost everything. Their reaction to being dumped (if they have any reaction at all) is surprise, as they had no idea that they were dating in the first place.

If you recognize any one of these as you (or people whom you have dated) you need Jeremial. He can break the cycle of patterns of behavior and make you think and act differently.

Tina "I used to date a lot of men. I guess you could say that I had a *Sex and the City* lifestyle. By the time I was thirty-seven I was totally disillusioned. I had been with a guy for two years and that Christmas he told me it was over. I thought, 'Right, that's it.' I decided that I was not going to look anymore. I had a nice house, great friends, and a good job. Why did I keep banging my head against a brick wall trying to make a relationship with a man work? I realized how unhappy I had been always looking for a man to share my life with. Now, I had so much more time. I could do so many things that I wanted. I joined a night school class once a week to learn pottery—something that I'd always wanted to do. Each week a group of us would sneak outside during the coffee break for a cigarette. As the weeks went by the smokers went from eight to just two—me and this nice guy. I began to admit to myself that I was now looking forward to Wednesday night's class and it had nothing whatsoever to do with the pottery. At the end of the course he asked me out for a drink. Last summer we got married and any day now I will be giving birth to his baby."

If at first you don't succeed ... you failed. It may seem like a good idea to keep trying again, but this is really a triumph of hope over experience. A better idea would be to work out why things went wrong with your past relationship and decide what you can do differently next time. You need to be brave to take stock of what has happened and the role that you played in it, but with Jeremial's help this is easy to do. He can make you see the lessons that you were meant to learn and how you can change and grow. Any behavior that was less than good for you he will point out, so that you can avoid it in the future.

Ask Jeremial to be with you as you look back at your relationship. He will give you the wisdom to see beyond the emotion that you felt at the time and understand the mistakes that were made. Seven is an angel number and there are seven common mistakes that people make when they set out angel dating. Put one hand on your heart and see if you ought to hold the other hand up to any of these.

Fault 1. You didn't really know yourself well enough. You set out dating before you had a clear idea of your own personality and preferences. Maybe you were not completely honest with your answers in Chapters One and Two and so created a flattering image of yourself.

How to fix it. Revisit Chapter One with the intention of being ruthlessly honest. Closely examine everything that makes you who you really are. Nobody has to see it but you, so tell your own truth.

Fault 2. You had unrealistic expectations for the relationship. You know that Raphael wanted you to have positive intentions, but you let false expectations creep in anyhow. Sneakily you were hoping for that knight on a white horse or that nymphomaniac supermodel who owns a football team. Consequently, anyone you met had difficulty living up to your high ideals.

How to fix it. Get real. If you keep playing out of your league you will always be playing solitaire. Accept that falling in love is an act of equalizing—of finding someone as great as you, not infinitely better.

Fault 3. You didn't listen to the angels. Okay, you had a vague notion that you ought to be doing this or that, but you dismissed it as just your imagination and carried on doing your own thing. You made mistakes because you didn't open yourself up to angelic guidance.

How to fix it. You can ask for help to open up and be receptive. Let those niggling thoughts take root and grow into big ideas. Know that when something is bothering you it is doing so for a reason, then take the time to find out what that reason is. You can even visit an angel counselor or other spiritual worker to help the process.

Fault 4. You didn't trust the angels. Even when you did hear the angels you didn't trust them to be right, so you disregarded their advice and made your own mistakes. This is as common as it is frustrating. We always think that we know better, until it is too late.

How to fix it. Drop the attitude. Infinite messengers of light will always know more than you, so do everyone a favor and have the humility to take their good advice when it comes your way. Now that you realize that angel guidance is always loving and always right, you can rely on it much more.

Fault 5. You stopped the angels from helping you. Whether you were aware of it or not, you blocked Chamuel's efforts to make you take a risk. You put reasons and walls of negativity in the way to protect yourself. A great chance of love and happiness may have passed you by because you didn't want to get hurt.

How to fix it. Now you can see that nobody suffered from this except you, so in future you can drop your defences. Chamuel's only desire is to help and bring you happiness, so let him take you by the hand down lovers' lane.

Fault 6. You didn't know what you wanted. You wasted time, effort, and emotion on the wrong person, because either you weren't honest with your Raphael List or you forgot all about it and didn't use it when you went dating.

How to fix it. You can return to your Raphael List with the benefit of a little experience. Are there some things that you would like to change in light of the romance that you have been through?

Jeremial can help you review your Raphael List and change things if necessary. If wealth was high on your list and you dated a rich but terribly cruel person, you may now have altered your priorities and replaced wealth with kindness. This type of adjustment is not unusual. Many people discover that what they thought they wanted isn't what they wanted at all, but they only find out by trial and error. Just don't keep changing your mind (and your list) every day. It is about getting to understand yourself better, not confusing yourself more.

Angel Advice
signs that you are ready to date again

1 You start finding the most unlikely people attractive.

2 You buy new underwear for no reason.

3 You look forward to the weekend again.

4 Angel wings flutter in your stomach.

5 You smile at strangers.

6 Strangers smile at you.

7 You're not afraid anymore.

Fault 7. You let fear win. The opposite of love is never hate, it is always fear. There is a huge difference between being single and happy and being single and scared. If you are happy being single for all the reasons that we looked at in Chapter One, if you are relieved that you are out of that relationship (or any relationship) and feel that this dating thing is not for you and you really want to be alone, then good for you. However, if you are terrified of all that love involves—losing independence, privacy, space; sharing thoughts, feelings, finances, bodies; risking rejection, embarrassment, heartache; coping with emotions, arguments, needs, expectations; living with and for another human being who can and might leave you—then you really do need help—angel help—and lots of it.

How to fix it. The biggest difference that Jeremial can make to your life is to rid you of fear. Fear is the most pervasive and corrosive of all our emotions. It sneaks up on you from behind and suddenly you are in its grip. Fear can stop you from doing things, going places, meeting people, dreaming, aspiring, taking risks, and falling in love. It can paralyze and destroy. It can convince you that black is white and something unreal is real. Fear itself is not real. The only thing that makes it real is your belief in it. Fear is like a check; it is only valid if it can be cashed. If J.K. Rowling writes a check for $1 million it is valid. If I write a check for $1 million it is only worth the paper it is written on. Always examine your fear against the reality of the situation to see if it is valid; if it isn't, then there is nothing to fear. Fear can stop you from doing many things, but don't let it stop you from falling in love.

Ask Jeremial to help you find out why and of what you are so afraid. Is it the fear of rejection, betrayal, being hurt, or losing control, or even the fear of success and being in a relationship? If you can pin down the reason, you can start to conquer it. As you created your fear in the first place you also have the power to destroy it. This may seem impossible but nothing is impossible to the angels, so you have only to ask Jeremial and he will give you the power to defeat anything. Freeing yourself from the hold that fear has over you allows you to love again.

Dismantling the old makes way for the new and when Jeremial is involved the "new" will always be better than the old. Jeremial's talent is to turn a supposed disaster into a wondrous opportunity. So what appeared so unbearable once will begin to seem unimportant now as Jeremial helps you to "get over it." He will prepare your heart for love again by reviewing your last relationship and helping you to understand what happened and why. You will begin to remove yourself from the emotion that was once so strong. At some point you will be happy to open that box of mementos and release those feelings (even if this means digging up an azalea bush).

When you are ready, Jeremial will hand you back to Archangel Michael, who will give you the courage to be vulnerable again. This is harder to do if you have been hurt in the past, but finding the courage to open up and trust again is possible. There is no need to take "baggage" with you, as you can check it in and

Angels *do* find us in our hour of *need*.

AMY HUFFMAN

leave it at the lost-luggage depot if you want. Michael (the warrior angel) is often depicted with a sword and he can use this to cut any ties that you still have to your old love. If you are still attached to someone by strong feelings Michael can sever these connections so that you are free to form new ones. When you can bless your old love and thank them for all that they gave and taught you, then you are ready to move on to a new love.

Gina "My world fell apart when my boyfriend left me for another woman. I was so sad that I could hardly go on. I prayed to the angels to help me and get me through this terrible time. I asked them to send me a sign that they had heard my prayers. I knew about finding feathers if the angels are with you but I was in such a state that I said I would need a bloody big bird. I did a deal with Archangel Michael and said that if he sent me a big bird I would know that he was looking after me. What happened next is truly incredible. After another night of crying myself to sleep I opened the curtains the next morning and saw a huge white swan in my garden. It must have found its way there from the river half a mile away. I knew it was a sign and Michael was telling me that he would give me the strength to go on."

Angels and dating—what's that all about? You may have started to read this book thinking that it was all a bit cuckoo. I mean, angels aren't even real, and even if they were what would they know about dating? It's not as if Archangel Gabriel has ever sat through a three-hour dinner with someone supremely dull, or Michael has ever had his pride shredded by a leggy brunette. And yet, if you only accept that angels are very real you can start to benefit from the wondrous effect that they can have on your life. Angels are all around us and ready to help with anything from a parking space to a love affair. All it takes is a little willingness on your part—a willingness to give them the nod that they have been waiting for to get involved. Like you, I thought all this was a bit mad, until I witnessed the amazing change that angel power made to my life and the lives of many others ... After all, what have you got to lose?

Dating is a dangerous business. There are so many ways to get hurt that it should be classed as an extreme sport. The sensible thing is to avoid it completely, stay sitting on top of that cliff and watch all the lemmings throw themselves off. But since when has sense had anything to do with love? When love knocks on the door, sense jumps out of the window. Who wants to be sensible anyway? There are many ways that you can live your life to the fullest and one of these is to share it with someone else. For all its difficulties love inspires, enhances, gives purpose, and makes you better than you ever thought you could be. Love is a gift that you deserve, and dating is when you get to unwrap it. If you stay on that cliff edge you will never know what the gift is like. The two saddest words in the universe are "what if." So go on, take a running jump off the cliff, fall in love, and let the angels help you to fly.

We are *each* of us angels with only *one* wing,

and we can only fly by *embracing* one another.

LUCIANO DE CRESCENZO

AUTHOR'S ACKNOWLEDGEMENTS

My heartfelt thanks go to everyone who believed in me and in this book, especially Anne Furniss and the hardworking team at Quadrille; my family for putting up with me; all the Pennos and Clarks for their love and support; my lovely friends including Rachael Billington, Lotte Bond, Trish Bertram, Eric Robinson, Jennifer Robinson, Gloria Varty, Frances Gainsley; and to my amazing husband Gordon for his unfailing strength and the precious gift of his love. Unfathomable thanks go to my mum and dad, Margie and Dickie, who inspired me by their limitless ability to love. Finally, big thanks to you for reading this book and to the angels for all that they do.

This edition first published in 2008 by Quadrille Publishing

Project editor Anne Furniss
Text editor Nicki Marshall
Design Claire Peters
Production Rebecca Short

© Text Laura Penn 2005
© Illustrations Matthew Usmar Lauder 2005
© Layout and design Quadrille Publishing Limited 2005

ISBN 978 184400 576 5
Printed and bound in China

Library of Congress Cataloging-in-Publication Data

Penn, Laura.
  The angels' guide to love and dating / Laura Penn ; illustrations by
Matthew Usmar Lauder.
     p. cm.
  ISBN 978-1-84400-576-5 (hardcover)
  1. Dating (Social customs) 2. Man-woman relationships. 3. Mate
selection. I. Title.
  HQ801.P3724 2008
  306.73088'20215--dc22
                              2007029182